"From the very first episode of the *You're N[...]* overarching theme of the podcast, and now [...] meant to produce gospel culture through which the church shines forth the beauty of Christ. I have come to embrace that message wholeheartedly and am thankful that Ray Ortlund and Sam Allberry have made it accessible to all through this book. If you're currently leading a church or ministry, or planning to do so in the future, this book is for you."

Brian Brodersen, Pastor, Calvary Chapel Costa Mesa, California

"This is the most important book I've read this year. *You're Not Crazy* is written for pastors, ministry leaders, and followers of Jesus who not only believe the gospel but also desire to experience good news in their everyday life and work. The grace of God should shape not merely our theology but also our experience within our churches. This is exactly what Ray Ortlund and Sam Allberry do through these biblically rich and deeply practical chapters. This book is refreshment for those who are weary, renewal for those who are disenchanted, clarity for those who are frustrated with the present state of the church, and rocket fuel for those who refuse to bow to the tribalism and outrage addiction of our times. Here you will find the kind of Christianity that every follower of Jesus longs deep down to experience. Read it slowly. Read it annually."

Adam Ramsey, Lead Pastor, Liberti Church, Gold Coast, Australia; Director, Acts 29 Asia Pacific; author, *Truth on Fire* and *Faithfully Present*

"*You're Not Crazy* contains an insightful, straightforward path toward seeing gospel culture established in your ministry—a path that travels through the very heart of Christ. Ray Ortlund and Sam Allberry's writing is quintessentially moving, motivating, and practical, as one would expect from two men who have lived their message so wholeheartedly. I wish I had read this fifteen years ago, and I can't recommend it highly enough."

Simon Murphy, Lead Pastor, Redemption Hill Church, Singapore

"In this book, Ray Ortlund and Sam Allberry unfold a biblical and beautiful truth: sound doctrine ought to create compelling community for followers of Jesus. The local church is Christianity enfleshed, and our life together is integral to our witness. The authors show how gospel doctrine creates gospel culture in various areas of church life—from the pastoral welcome, to how we honor one another, to how we preach, and more. Here is a timely and inspirational reminder to turn afresh to the high calling of being part of—and helping foster—the body of Christ."

Samuel D. Ferguson, Rector, The Falls Church Anglican, Metro Washington, DC

"A church that lacks gospel culture will undermine its gospel preaching. A gospel culture welcomes messed-up people to stumble toward glory together, knowing that God's grace is their only hope. *You're Not Crazy* is an invitation for Christians and churches to press past the confusion of our day and experience the beauty of Jesus's grace together. I highly commend this work."

J. Garrett Kell, Pastor, Del Ray Baptist Church, Alexandria, Virginia; author, *Pure in Heart: Sexual Sin and the Promises of God*

"Huge, if true! As I read this book, named after the authors' hugely popular podcast, line after line hit me with life-giving gospel hope. In fact, I started sending quotes over to my wife but soon realized I was effectively texting her the whole book. What a tragedy that so many who declare or defend gospel doctrine have failed to develop gospel culture. What damage this has done to Christ's body and witness. And what an incredible tonic this book will be for those committed afresh to moving truths from head to heart to life."

Dave Gobbett, Lead Pastor, Highfields Church, Cardiff; author, *The Environment*; Trustee, Word Alive

"I love this book. I love it for exploring God's vision in his word for gospel doctrine to create a gospel culture in our churches. I love how it applies precious gospel truths like grace, justification, and glorification to honesty, hospitality, and honoring in church life. I love how it explores God's vision for the preaching, leadership, and relationships in our church families, which is so compelling to the communities we're trying to reach. I love it because it encourages and challenges Western evangelical churches—rocked by leadership scandals, denominational revisionism, and class tribalism—to rediscover God's inspiring vision for his churches in which the love of Christ truly shapes and fuels our ministries and lives."

Richard Coekin, Senior Minister, Dundonald Church, London; Director, Co-Mission

You're Not Crazy

Other Crossway Books by Ray Ortlund and Sam Allberry

Ray Ortlund

The Death of Porn: Men of Integrity Building a World of Nobility

The Gospel: How the Church Portrays the Beauty of Christ

Isaiah: God Saves Sinners

Marriage and the Mystery of the Gospel

Proverbs: Wisdom That Works

Sam Allberry

7 Myths about Singleness

What God Has to Say about Our Bodies: How the Gospel Is Good News for Our Physical Selves

You're Not Crazy

Gospel Sanity for Weary Churches

Ray Ortlund and Sam Allberry

Foreword by Russell Moore
Afterword by Clark Lowenfield

CROSSWAY®

WHEATON, ILLINOIS

Library of Congress Cataloging-in-Publication Data

Names: Ortlund, Raymond C., Jr., author. | Allberry, Sam, author.
Title: You're not crazy : gospel sanity for weary churches / Ray Ortlund and Sam Allberry ; foreword by Dr. Russell Moore ; afterward by Bishop Clark Lowenfield.
Description: Wheaton, Illinois : Crossway, [2023] | Includes bibliographical references and index.
Identifiers: LCCN 2023005761 (print) | LCCN 2023005762 (ebook) | ISBN 9781433590573 (trade paperback) | ISBN 9781433590580 (pdf) | ISBN 9781433590597 (epub)
Subjects: LCSH: Clergy—Religious life.
Classification: LCC BV4011.6 .O78 2023 (print) | LCC BV4011.6 (ebook) | DDC 248.8/92—dc23/ eng/20230407
LC record available at https://lccn.loc.gov/2023005761
LC ebook record available at https://lccn.loc.gov/2023005762

To the Rev. Dr. T. J. Tims,
Friend and Pastor

Contents

Foreword

IN A CRAZY TIME, sanity seems insane. In an irrational time, reasonableness seems disloyal. In an angry time, peaceability seems provocative. We've seen this over and over again throughout history. Sometimes in order to keep your mind and your soul, you will feel as though you are all alone. That's often necessary. Sometimes God's call for you is to be the only one to say to injustice, "No," or to say to the invisible, "I see you," or to say to the mistreated, "I believe you."

And yet, though that willingness to stand alone is necessary for the sanity of any society or any family or any church, we also know that no one can withstand craziness alone—at least not forever.

A generation ago, sociologist Peter Berger wrote about the way that "plausibility structures" work[1]—the way that those taken-for-granted assumptions of the community around us can change not just what we believe but even what we *consider*:

> To deny reality as it is has been socially defined is to risk falling into irreality, because it is well-nigh impossible in the long run

1 Peter Berger, *The Sacred Canopy: Elements of a Sociological Theory of Religion* (1967; repr., New York: Knopf Doubleday, 1990), 39.

to keep up alone and without social support one's own counter-definitions of the world. When the socially defined reality has come to be identified with the ultimate reality of the universe, then its denial takes on the quality of evil as well as madness.[2]

Much of the craziness of our time is the effort to skew the plausibility structures, sometimes even to force a kind of irrationality as a way to prove one's loyalty to the tribe. If Berger is right, then our typical strategy—just waiting for the fever of that craziness to break—is dangerous not just to the individuals caught up in it but to future generations as well. After all, what is accepted as plausible in one generation—sometimes enforced by loyalty tests—becomes the default for generations to come.

That's why your ministry—whatever it is—is so important. You are not just serving the people in front of you at the moment. You are not just connecting isolated individuals to a community (although you are doing that). You are also connecting the community to reality, to a truth that is not "useful" but transcendent and personal. You are not just helping people to live their lives with flourishing and integrity (although you are doing that), but you are also pointing them to what they can't see, to what the anchor holds behind the veil (Heb. 6:19). When people face the ultimate moment of death, they do not need shibboleths that prove they are "one of us." They need to know "Is it true?" They need to know "Is he there?"

That's why we need the word of God through which we hear the voice of Christ, through which we are conformed to that great

2 Berger, *Sacred Canopy*, 39.

community of believers from Abel to whoever first told you about Jesus to people living now but whose village you will never see and whose language you will never learn.

When you start to wonder whether you're crazy, you are pulled in a couple of different directions. You might isolate and just start to live within your own mind. That, ultimately, leads to a seeking for sensations just to give some imitation of life. Or you might assimilate—taking on the untrue assertions of those around you because it's easier. If you practice the expected falsehoods long enough, you might even start to believe them. Both of those ways lead to despair, to exhaustion, and ultimately to collapse.

You are loved and valued, and we need you healthy and whole. The church needs you—whether or not you're in vocational ministry—not to be paralyzed by self-questioning and a failure of nerve. That's why this book is important.

Ray Ortlund and Sam Allberry are wise and respected leaders throughout the world, but some of us have been able to see them up close. We've seen them ministering in our local church—teaching the Bible, counseling the bewildered, serving the lonely. We've seen them take those who believed their ministries were over—very sane people who started to wonder whether they were "crazy"—and encourage them, pointing them to the sort of renewing of the mind and transfusing of hope that can come only from presence rooted in the word and enlivened by the Spirit.

This book will help you in your calling, steadying you for turbulent times, without hectoring you with preachy imperatives. This book is not "Do it more!" or "Do it better!" or "Do it like me!" This book is instead more like a couple of trusted friends who are saying, "You're not crazy; we see it too. You're not imagining how hard it is. And you're not wrong about how overwhelming it is. But here's what we've found, and here's how you can find it too."

Ultimately, that's not about "experts" teaching you "technique." That's what led so many churches and leaders to insanity in the first place. This approach is much more like those in first-century Galilee who heard a man speak like they'd never heard before, and who said to their friends, "Come meet this Jesus, from Nazareth. I can't really describe to you what he's like. Just come along with me, come and see."

The end result of that is the sort of sanity that's not just the absence of craziness, the sort of ministry that's not just the presence of "effectiveness." The end result is a personal encounter that the old hymns tell us about:

> Yes, 'tis sweet to trust in Jesus,
> Just from sin and self to cease;
> Just from Jesus simply taking
> Life and rest, and joy, and peace.[3]

You're not crazy. You're not forgotten. And you're not alone.

Russell Moore

EDITOR IN CHIEF

CHRISTIANITY TODAY

---

3 Louisa M. R. Stead, "'Tis So Sweet to Trust in Jesus" (1882), Hymnary.org, accessed December 15, 2022, https://hymnary.org/.

Introduction

LIKE MANY PEOPLE, I (Sam) use an app to keep track of my health. I make notes of my sleep quality, weight, exercise, and (if I'm really being diligent) my caloric intake. I can see all this at a glance and measure which way things are trending from week to week. It's been useful. I live with Crohn's disease, and these metrics give me a basic sense of how I'm doing. The trouble is, of course, all those metrics that I need to track for Crohn's could be going well but I could still be seriously unwell. After all, there's more than one way to be sick.

The same is true of our churches. I've had the privilege (a great privilege it is) of being in theologically careful churches for the whole of my Christian life. I don't take this for granted. At each of these churches, the Scripture's authority drove all our ministries and teaching. We wanted to be biblical. In each case, the congregations were encouraged to listen to preaching with their Bibles open and to make sure what was being taught lined up with what was in the text. Teachers were always open to correction, and I continue to rejoice in the blessing of the many years I sat under their faithful and careful exposition.

But there's more than one way to be unhealthy. It's possible for any of us to be theologically careful and still be seriously sick. This first came home to me when I read through 1 Timothy and reflected on Paul's instructions for the care of widows:

> If a widow has children or grandchildren, let them first learn to show godliness to their own household and to make some return to their parents, for this is pleasing in the sight of God. She who is truly a widow, left all alone, has set her hope on God and continues in supplications and prayers night and day, but she who is self-indulgent is dead even while she lives. Command these things as well, so that they may be without reproach. But if anyone does not provide for his relatives, and especially for members of his household, he has denied the faith and is worse than an unbeliever. (1 Tim. 5:4–8)

Did you spot it? I don't know how many times I read this text without noticing it myself. In that last line, Paul shows that not providing for relatives isn't merely a serious sin of omission; it's a denial of the faith. I'd always seen denying the faith as a *theological* failure: At some point, someone starts to believe what is false, or he begins to deny what is true. He goes off the rails doctrinally. But here we see it's also possible to deny the faith *by what we do* (or, in this case, by what we don't do). It's entirely possible for someone who has never strayed theologically to *deny the faith* practically. But it's also possible for a whole church to affirm or deny the faith by either embodying it or failing to do so. That's why we have written this book.

We humans are culture creators. How we are around each other will always take on a particular relational dynamic, a shared personality, a noticeable tone. It can never be otherwise. We shape one another in many complex ways, and a resulting culture always emerges. It's true of friendship groups, of workplaces, of families, and of churches. There will always be a vibe, a feel, an intangible but powerful way the group tends to *be* when together.

Every church has its own culture. The question is, How fully does its culture align with its doctrine? Whatever the answer, a church's culture always reveals whatever the people most deeply believe. Not every truth that's preached is believed down at the level of felt, shared reality. Some truths are given lip service, while others become deeply defining. The sorting process isn't always visible, but the outcomes will show themselves in a church's observable culture.

A pastor friend once said that it may be safer to confess sin in the bars and clubs of his city than in its churches. This shouldn't be. If the members of a church are merely keeping up appearances, if they, for instance, fear opening up about their sins and failings, those gospel truths aren't yet believed down at the level where the church's culture is formed. A church may formally believe in the forgiveness of sins and in the freedom of confession—its sermons and liturgy may affirm that grace for sin is abundantly available— but while this church seems healthy at the level of doctrine, it may be seriously unhealthy at the level of culture. To use Paul's stark language, they may be denying the faith they profess to believe. That is how the people in a church can affirm glorious theology but be weary in their hearts and in their witness.

That's a negative way to frame what our book is about. And let's all face that stark reality. But there is a positive message here too. We're longing for the beauty of Christ to shape every aspect of our churches—not only the content of our teaching but also the quality and flavor of our relationships. We believe that the culture of our churches, empowered by the doctrine of our churches, can make the presence of the risen Jesus a felt reality in this generation.

So, our plan in this book is to establish what we mean by "gospel culture" in our churches and to make a biblical case for why this is essential (chapter 1). Then, in the remaining chapters, we will (broadly) follow an order of service and think together about how we might try to reflect the beautifying impact of the gospel from our opening welcome to the way we're sent out at the service's end. On the way, we'll cover the vital ingredients of honesty, honor, preaching, leadership, and mission, and we'll think through what it might look like to make all this more "Jesus-y."

This is the ministry that Scripture itself is calling all of us to. We ourselves have been struck by how full the category of *faith-fulness* really is. It's not gospel doctrine alone, but gospel doctrine creating gospel culture. The truth of Christ must shape our creeds and our sermons *so that* the beauty of Christ also adorns our life together as churches. Then we will be a prophetic presence in the world today.

What Is Gospel Culture, and Why Does It Matter?

*To them we did not yield in submission
even for a moment, so that the truth of the
gospel might be preserved for you.*

GALATIANS 2:5

HOW GOSPEL DOCTRINE connects to gospel culture became clear for me (Sam) when I ran into a long-standing church member at the store.[1] We had one short conversation, but it was emblematic of a much wider concern. She'd been going through a crisis, and we hadn't seen her at church for a few weeks, which was unlike her. So when I ran into her, I told her how much we'd missed her

---

1 Some content in this chapter is adapted from Ray Ortlund, "Justification versus Self-Justification," a talk given at the TGC National Conference, April 13, 2011. Available online at https://media.thegospelcoalition.org/static-blogs/ray-ortlund/files/2011/04/TGClecture.pdf.

and how lovely it would be to see her in church again. She told me she couldn't come until she was doing better. She didn't want people to see her while she was feeling life's mess: "I'm waiting until the storm passes and I've got things back together enough to be able to walk back into the church building."

Her words were heartbreaking to hear. In her mind, church was a place she could come only when she felt like her life was together. She didn't even identify this as a problem. It was just reality for her. I saw in that moment that there was something unhealthy going on. Church should be the place we sprint to when things are at their worst, not the place we avoid until we've got our Instagram-worthy Christianity back in place.

I began to realize that there was a mismatch between the beauty of the truth and the culture of my church. The more I thought about it, the more clearly I saw the difference between the social dynamics of grace-justification and the social dynamics of self-justification.

We all need to examine this so we can enlarge our understanding of what it means to be faithful to the gospel. Yes, even the social dynamics of the gospel matter because, as Luther taught us, justification by faith alone is not just one doctrine among others; it is "the article by which the church stands or falls."[2] Luther also teaches us that justification by faith alone is hard to accept and hard to hold on to. In his commentary on Galatians, he writes,

2 Martin Luther, *Luthers Werke: Kritische Gesamtausgabe* [Schriften], 73 vols. (Weimar: H. Böhlau, 1883–2009), 40/3.352.3. Literally, "Because if this article [of justification] stands, the church stands; if this article collapses, the church collapses." See Justin Taylor, "Luther's Saying: 'Justification Is the Article by Which the Church Stands and Falls,'" *Between Two Worlds* (blog), The Gospel Coalition (website), August 31, 2011, https:// www.thegospelcoalition.org. Translations by Carl Trueman, whom Taylor credits.

[This doctrine] cannot be beaten into our ears enough or too much. Yes, though we learn it and understand it well, yet there is no one that takes hold of it perfectly or believes it with all his heart, so frail a thing is our flesh and disobedient to the Spirit.[3]

Based on Galatians, then, the gospel—and justification in particular—calls for more than doctrinal subscription. It also calls for cultural incarnation. It's not necessarily easy to follow through at both levels. It's impossible without Christ himself. But we would be unfaithful to settle for doctrinal correctness without also establishing a culture of grace in our churches and denominations and movements. In other words, if justification by faith alone is the doctrine on which the church stands or falls, what does it look like to stand rather than fall? Is it possible to fall while we think we are standing?

The book of Galatians and my conversation at the store show us that such confusion is possible. A believer or a church can trumpet the doctrine of grace-justification while, at the same time, being crippled with the dysfunctions of self-justification. In Galatians, Paul is pressing the gospel forward at both levels simultaneously—the doctrine and the culture. He couldn't be satisfied if the Galatians' only response to his letter would be to reassert justification by faith alone as a doctrine; it's clear from this letter that he also expects them to establish a church culture consistent with that doctrine. That, in Paul's view, is what it means to be faithful to Christ.

---

3 Martin Luther, *A Commentary on St. Paul's Epistle to the Galatians: Based on Lectures Delivered at the University of Wittenberg, in the Year 1531 and First Published in 1535* (London: James Clarke, 1953), 40. Compare pages 56, 61, and 101. Style updated.

And that's the appeal we're making in this book. We will clarify it in this chapter and then develop it further in the rest of the book. We believe that the New Testament expects and helps our churches to nurture healthy church cultures consistent with their life-giving gospel doctrine. To make this case, this chapter proposes three theological convictions and then briefly unpacks three biblical passages.

Three Convictions

First, the classical Protestant doctrine of justification by grace alone through faith alone in Christ alone, apart from all our works, is the truth. Article 11 of the Thirty-Nine Articles declares it clearly:

> We are accounted righteous before God only for the merit of our Lord and Savior Jesus Christ, by faith, and not for our own works or deservings. Wherefore, that we are justified by faith only is a most wholesome doctrine and very full of comfort.[4]

This articulation of the doctrine reminds us of the objectivity, the exteriority, the *out-there-ness*, the *Someone-Else-ness* of our justification, as John Bunyan also reminds us in his *Grace Abounding*:

> One day as I was passing into the field, and that too with some dashes on my conscience, fearing lest all was still not right, suddenly this sentence fell upon my soul, "Thy righteousness is in

---

4 Thirty-Nine Articles of Religion, in *The Creeds of Christendom*, vol. 3, ed. Philip Schaff (1877; repr., Grand Rapids, MI: Baker, 1990), 494.

heaven." And I thought I saw, with the eyes of my soul, Jesus Christ at God's right hand, there, I say, as my righteousness; so that wherever I was or whatever I was doing, God could not say of me, "He lacks my righteousness," for that [righteousness] was right before Him. I also saw that it was not my good frame of heart that made my righteousness better, nor my bad frame that made my righteousness worse, for my righteousness was Jesus Christ Himself, "the same yesterday and today and forever." Now did my chains fall off my legs indeed. . . . Now I went home rejoicing for the grace and love of God. . . . Here therefore I lived, for some time, very sweetly at peace with God through Christ. Oh, I thought, Christ! Christ! There was nothing but Christ before my eyes.[5]

Second, self-justification is the deepest impulse in the fallen human heart. We might sincerely agree with the biblical doctrine of justification by faith alone. But deep in our hearts, it isn't that simple, is it? Gerhard Forde helps us see ourselves:

The problem lies in the fact that the Old Being will not and cannot *hear* gospel no matter what one says. The Old Being will only use whatever is said as part of the protection, solidification in the *causa sui* project [the self-justifications we build], and translate it into or see it as a ratification of the legal system. That is, the Old Being will turn *whatever one says* into law.[6]

---

5 John Bunyan, *The Complete Works of John Bunyan* (Philadelphia: Bradley, Garretson, 1873), 59; style updated.

6 Gerhard O. Forde, *Justification by Faith: A Matter of Death and Life* (Philadelphia: Fortress, 1982), 92.

We deeply desire to save ourselves. Legalism is our native tongue. At the same time, our sin includes a hidden filter blocking out clarity about our sin. Martyn Lloyd-Jones describes our lack of self-awareness:

> You will never make yourself feel that you are a sinner, because there is a mechanism in you as a result of sin that will always be defending you against every accusation. We are all on very good terms with ourselves, and we can always put up a good case for ourselves. Even if we try to make ourselves feel that we are sinners, we will never do it. There is only one way to know that we are sinners, and that is to have some dim, glimmering conception of God.[7]

Our mentality of blind self-justification makes Paul's letter to the Galatians endlessly relevant to us believers. The Puritan William Fenner teaches us to see justification by faith alone as a constant resource:

> As we sin daily, so he justifies daily, and we must daily go to him for it. . . . Justification is an ever-running fountain, and therefore we cannot look to have all the water at once.[8]

Justification by our own righteousness is not a Galatian problem only, or a Catholic problem only; it is a human problem

---

7 Martyn Lloyd-Jones, *Seeking the Face of God: Nine Reflections on the Psalms* (1991; repr., Wheaton, IL: Crossway, 2005), 34.

8 William Fenner, quoted in J. I. Packer, *A Quest for Godliness: The Puritan Vision of the Christian Life* (Wheaton, IL: Crossway, 1990), 115; spelling modernized.

universally. It's a *Christian* problem. It's our problem. You and I are always, at best, an inch away from its dark powers. Indeed, it is possible to preach and defend the doctrine of justification by grace alone but out of motives of self-justification—and to do so with its bitter fruit. This kind of disconnect leads to bad things, even in churches that sincerely love the Lord.

Third, gospel doctrine creates gospel culture. When the gospel is taught clearly, and when the people of a church believe it deeply, it does more than renew us personally. The doctrine of grace also creates a *culture* of grace. In such a church, the gospel is both articulated at the obvious level of doctrine and embodied at the subtle level of vibe, ethos, feel, relationships, and community. In a gospel-shaped church, for starters, people are honest in confession, bear one another's burdens, and seek to outdo one another in showing honor.

But because of our second conviction—the power of our self-justifying impulses—getting and keeping both gospel doctrine and gospel culture in a church is difficult. Without the doctrine, the culture is unsustainable. Without the culture, the doctrine appears pointless. But really believing the gospel together requires deep change. We can be like the Pharisee described in Luke 18:9–14: "Jesus also told this parable to some who trusted in themselves that they were righteous, and treated others with contempt" (18:9). The evangelist then recounts Jesus's parable. In the Savior's story, a Pharisee went to the temple, the place of substitutionary atonement. Why? He believed in it. But his heart was more devious than his belief. The Pharisee's self-justifying heart spilled over in an attitude of contempt toward the tax collector. Self-justification creates an outlook of aloofness, superiority, negative scrutiny, and

"Gotcha!" Though we hold to the doctrine of grace-justification, our deeper thoughts and feelings can slip into functional self-justification, and it shows.

Trusting in ourselves that we're righteous and viewing others with contempt always go together. When we notice ourselves drifting into dismissive contempt, there is always a reason: a gospel deficit in our heart, however sincere the gospel profession in our head. We look at our doctrinal statements and our mental beliefs, and they seem to line up. But a tip-off that the gospel doesn't yet have as deep a hold on us as we wish is whenever, like this Pharisee, we start looking for someone to judge, someone onto whom we can project our own guilty anxiety. If we need a scapegoat to preserve our own okay-ness, we aren't really trusting in the perfect scapegoat that God provided at the cross. And a blame-shifting heart creates a culture of ugliness toward others. Justification by faith alone, by contrast, creates a culture of acceptance, warmth, beauty, and safety. As Paul encouraged the Romans, "Therefore welcome one another as Christ has welcomed you, for the glory of God" (Rom. 15:7). The more clearly the doctrine is taught, and the more beautifully that culture is nurtured, the more powerfully a church will bear prophetic witness to Jesus as the mighty friend of sinners.

Three Key Passages

In recent years here in the US, we've seen a wonderful resurgence of gospel doctrine. I (Ray) went through my own gospel renaissance about twenty years ago, while preaching through Romans at First Presbyterian Church in Augusta, Georgia. I rediscovered justification by faith alone, imputed righteousness, and Jesus as our substitute. These great doctrines are right at the center of the gospel, and I found them thrilling. Our church felt like we were going through the wardrobe into Narnia as we saw Jesus in his grace and glory with fresh eyes. Many of us have been enriched, strengthened, and helped in recent years as the truth of the gospel has been clarified among us. But I can't see that we TGC types have experienced a corresponding resurgence in relational beauty. I don't know anyone who's downright mean. But I am convinced that the time has come to attend carefully, reverently, and joyously to building the intangibles of gospel culture that the doctrines themselves call for.

Paul in Galatians guides us in this direction—away from self-justification and toward grace-justification. Let's briefly consider three passages that introduce gospel culture.

First, in Galatians 1:10, we see that serving Christ frees us from groveling. Paul writes,

> For am I now seeking the approval of man, or of God? Or am I trying to please man? If I were still trying to please man, I would not be a servant of Christ. (Gal. 1:10)

Why does Paul say that? He has just heaped anathemas on anyone who teaches a false gospel. Apparently, some had accused Paul of being a cowardly people pleaser because of his message of grace. Now he counters that accusation, effectively saying, "My anathemas in verses 8–9: Would a compromiser make such statements?"

But what is the gospel doctrine he embeds in 1:10, and how does Paul himself demonstrate the way it works out in gospel culture? The doctrine implicit in Paul's declaration—that his heart is set on God's approval—is the all-sufficiency of Christ, a doctrine necessary to justification by faith alone.

Paul's view of Christ is high, reverent, uncluttered. Christ is the only one whose judgment finally matters. All Christians believe that. We believe that our personal validation comes not from ourselves or from other sinners but only from Christ. His approval alone is enough for us. That gospel conviction creates a culture of boldly independent nobility of mind, such as we see in Paul.

Paul cares intensely about people. He cares sincerely about their feelings, and he wants to please them. He says in 1 Corinthians 10:33, "I try to please *everyone* in *everything* I do." What a sweetheart this man is! He's widely adaptable because he respects people and their various ways of seeing things. How does he reconcile his desire to please people, on the one hand, with his deeper desire to please God, on the other?

When Paul faces a choice between pleasing himself and pleasing others, he pleases others. When he faces a choice between pleasing others and pleasing God, he pleases God. In fact, he's so clear about this that he states his position as a stark either-or: "If I were still trying to please man, I would not be a servant of Christ" (Gal 1:10). He will not depart from Christ for anyone. His justification is in Christ alone, and to Christ alone he therefore gives himself in complete surrender, whatever price he might pay in human disapproval. Paul wants to please people for the sake of Christ, but he wants to please Christ more, so he's willing to be unpopular, even controversial. He is willing to be misunderstood and misjudged. He doesn't relish it. But neither is he threatened by it. And by his example, he's calling the Galatians and us to follow him into the kind of trust in Christ alone that frees us from craving human approval too much.

That's the first indicator of gospel doctrine getting traction in our hearts. It's us trusting in Christ alone, even when people misjudge us. The ultimacy of Christ does not position us to go with the crowd, not even the Christian crowd, as if we need Christ *plus human applause* to stand on our own two feet.

In his brilliant essay on justification by faith alone, J. Gresham Machen rightly calls this doctrine

> an answer to the greatest personal question ever asked by a human soul—the question, "How shall I be right with God? How do I stand in God's sight? With what favor does he look upon me?" There are those, I admit, who never raise that question; there are those who are concerned with the question of their standing before men but never with the question of their standing before God; there are those who are interested in what "people say" but not in the question of what God says. Such men, however, are not those who move the world; they are apt to go with the current; they are apt to do as others do; they are not the heroes who change the destinies of the race. *The beginning of true nobility comes when a man ceases to be interested in the judgment of men and becomes interested in the judgment of God.*[9]

It is so freeing to stop itching for human recognition. It is so freeing to get up and follow Christ, though inevitably some will find fault. It is so freeing to be that deeply bound to Jesus. If he

9   J. Gresham Machen, *God Transcendent* (1949; repr., Edinburgh: Banner of Truth, 1982), 89–90; emphasis added.

is all our justification, all our okay-ness, then we can hold our heads high. The doctrine of justification creates a culture filled with noble servants of Christ who can think for themselves. Pastors like that can change the course of history.

Second, in Galatians 2:11–14, we see that trusting Christ emboldens us to fight oppression. Paul writes,

> But when Cephas came to Antioch, I opposed him to his face, because he stood condemned. For before certain men came from James, he was eating with the Gentiles; but when they came he drew back and separated himself, fearing the circumcision party. The rest of the Jews acted hypocritically along with him, so that even Barnabas was led astray by their hypocrisy. But when I saw that their conduct was not in step with the truth of the gospel, I said to Cephas before them all, "If you, though a Jew, live like a Gentile and not like a Jew, how can you force the Gentiles to live like Jews?"

This passage alerts us to the danger of absolutizing mere tradition. Peter did that, and Paul calls him out for it. There is nothing wrong with holiness located in Jewish traditions. But there is something wrong with absolutizing and enforcing that tradition because Christ fulfills the ritual laws of Moses. When Peter distances himself from the unkosher Gentile believers, he is, in effect, throwing redemptive history into reverse gear. What is he saying by his behavior? He's saying that Gentile believers must adapt to Jewish culture for them to be good enough for Jesus—and for Peter! What an insult to the finished work of Christ on the cross. How demeaning to those Gentile believers. What an abuse of the book of Leviticus. What an arrogant exaltation of Peter's traditional sensitivities. What a violation of justification by faith alone. And what a pathetic church culture.

And Peter knew better. God had taught Peter, through the vision of the sheet coming down with the unclean animals, that "what God has made clean, do not call common" (Acts 10:15). So here in Antioch, what drives Peter is not ignorance, nor a deeper insight into the gospel, but fear—fear of church politics, fear of being disinvited to preach at future conferences in Jerusalem: "He drew back and separated himself, fearing the circumcision party." When Peter denied Jesus back in the gospels, he was panicking for his physical self-preservation. Here in Antioch, he's denying Jesus again, this time by panicking for his social self-preservation. Under that primitive fear, Peter falsified the gospel—not at the level of doctrine but at the level of culture. He was forcing these Gentile believers to conform to Jewish customs in order to be acceptable to God as full members of his church (Gal. 2:14).

Paul twice calls it hypocrisy (2:13). It feeds posturing, posing, wanting to be perceived in a certain way, and wanting to be identified with certain people or on a certain bandwagon. What is this fear, but the empty drivenness of self-justification?

Hypocrisy can be a powerful force among us Christians. Peter's hypocrisy was so contagious that even Barnabas was swept away. Paul alone had the courage to stand up and oppose Peter openly. We can be glad he did, because the gospel was at stake—the gospel for Galatia and for all of us everywhere. If Paul had caved along with Peter, the spread of the gospel would have stalled because the gospel would have been accessible only to those few people who could embrace Jewish Christianity as the best Christianity.

Earlier in the chapter, Paul wrote how, at another moment of decision, he took a bold stand "so that the truth of the gospel might be preserved for you" (Gal. 2:5). Both there and here in 2:14, Paul insists on the gospel as more than a bare theological datum. What does this tell us? It tells us faithfulness is more than saying, "Justification by faith alone is the truth." Faithfulness also follows through on the relational implications. If we today allow ourselves to be less than faithful, we unsay with our actions what we confess with our mouths.

But we might not notice, if all we do is look at the doctrine and think, "Of course that's what I believe." Peter knew what he believed too. Paul says in 2:16, "We [you and I, Peter] have believed in Christ Jesus, in order to be justified by faith." Peter never changed his doctrinal position. What he did was deconstruct the culture entailed in the doctrine. In 2:15–21, Paul goes on to show that Peter's behavior rebuilt the culture of self-justification he'd torn down (2:18). Peter's actions nullified the grace of God and desecrated Christ's cross (2:21). And Peter was an apostle! In fact, everyone involved in this sorry episode was a Christian believer. As we've said before, self-justification is a Christian problem. In Antioch, it was even an apostolic problem. Preserving the truth of the gospel in each generation is no simple matter. Let us never think we're above betraying the truth we love.

Galatians 2:11–14 pushes us to search ourselves with deeper questions. We must ask more than, Do we subscribe to the doctrine of justification by faith alone? We must also ask, Are we keeping in practical step with that doctrinal truth? Do we assess our faithfulness with *both* considerations? Paul included applying the gospel within his vision for faithfulness to the gospel: "I saw that their conduct was not in step with the truth of the gospel" (2:14). So now we know. The gospel is more than a place to stand. It's also a path to follow.

John Stott calls Paul's confrontation of Peter "without doubt one of the most tense and dramatic episodes in the New Testament."[10] Sometimes we can't change any other way. Paul's apostolic boldness helped Peter see the all-sufficient Christ with greater clarity, reconsider his behavior, and get back in step with how gracious God really is.

What, then, is the doctrine embedded in Galatians 2:11–14, and what kind of culture does that doctrine create? The doctrine is that everyone who simply trusts Jesus for their justification is clean before God, whatever their background. They don't need to add another layer of acceptability to man in addition to Christ's merit. If God declares us kosher through Christ alone, who can demand more? And the culture created by that doctrine is one of bold freedom and wide acceptability. Self-justification creates a culture of demanding oppression—though people passionately committed to Protestant doctrine can fall into it, as in fact Peter did. But Jesus said, "My yoke is easy" (Matt. 11:30).

What stands out to us about Galatians 2:11–14 is that Paul considers gospel culture just as sacred as gospel doctrine. He fought for that culture because the doctrine of grace-justification cannot be preserved in its integrity if it is surrounded by a culture of self-justification.

Finally, in Galatians 4:17, we see that sensitivity to Christ makes us alert to selfishness. Paul writes of the legalistic false teachers:

10 John R. W. Stott, *Only One Way: The Message of Galatians* (London: Inter-Varsity Press, 1968), 49.

They make much of you, but for no good purpose. They want to shut you out, that you may make much of them.

And then in 5:15, he warns the Galatians themselves,

But if you bite and devour one another, watch out that you are not consumed by one another.

These verses clarify for us the negative dynamics unleashed into a church by the mentality of self-justification. What kind of dark church culture emerges when a gospel culture doesn't? One of *selfish ambition* and *savage destruction*.

Galatians 4:17 exposes the manipulative power of exclusion. "They make much of you" can be paraphrased, "They are zealous for you. They are eager to win you over. They take such an interest in you. They seem to care about you so deeply." The false teachers appeared loving and concerned. But they had an ulterior motive. It was like chapter 2 in *The Adventures of Tom Sawyer*. Tom wanted to go fishing. But Aunt Polly had told him to whitewash the back fence. So Tom tricked a pal of his into doing the job for him by the clever power of exclusion. Mark Twain wrote, "In order to make a man or boy covet a thing, it is only necessary to make the thing difficult to attain."[11] But full inclusion in the church of Christ is easy to attain! All we need is Christ. And he gives himself away freely, on terms of grace. Our only part is to lift the empty hands of faith.

To accomplish their hidden purpose, the false teachers had to get Paul out of the way. They therefore encouraged a sense

11 Mark Twain, *The Adventures of Tom Sawyer* (1876; repr., New York: Harper and Brothers, 1903), 33.

of grievance against Paul, making him an enemy (4:16). If the legalists could blur the people's hyperfocus on Christ—and Paul was a barrier to that purpose—then they could take control. So, they redefined acceptability within Galatian Christianity on their own fraudulent terms. The people, in their weakness, were falling for their false doctrine and conforming to their oppressive culture. Without a return to the good news of Christ crucified for unwashed sinners like us all, the heretics would own those churches as their own religious sandboxes to play in, their reign unchallenged. John Calvin comments,

> This stratagem is common to all the ministers of Satan, of alienating the people from their pastor, to draw them [the people] to themselves [the false teachers] and having, so to say, disposed of the rival, to take his place.[12]

Paul is so disturbed by what the Galatians themselves cannot see that when he takes pen in hand at the end of the letter, he adds this:

> It is those who want to make a good showing in the flesh who would force you to be circumcised. . . . They desire to have you circumcised that they may boast in your flesh. (Gal. 6:12–13)

In other words, the heretics wanted to use the Galatians to en-hance their own professional big-deal-ness. It was self-justification

---

12 John Calvin, *The Epistles of Paul the Apostle to the Galatians, Ephesians, Philippians and Colossians*, ed. David W. Torrance and Thomas F. Torrance, trans. T. H. L. Parker (Grand Rapids, MI: Eerdmans, 1980), 82.

by numbers of conversions—and not conversions to Christ for his true glory but to their group for their own smug glory. Their behavior was the *opposite* of what Paul required of himself back in Galatians 1, when he refused to compromise the gospel for the sake of human approval. He was a servant of Christ. The false teachers were promoters of self.

That self-devotion could lead only to savage destruction: "But if you bite and devour one another, watch out that you are not consumed by one another." How does an animal bite and devour its victims? With its mouth. The sins of the tongue can destroy a church's worship, fellowship, and witness.

The Galatian churches were unstable to begin with. The reassuring finality of "It is finished" had been eroded away by the acids of legalism. And self-justification creates only a howling demand that nothing outside Christ can satisfy. No matter how well a person has been raised to be courteous, legalism must generate finger-pointing, accusing, slandering, and dividing. Whatever the outcome, no one wins.

When savagery erupts in any church, whether from the congregation or from the leadership, the problem is not a lack of niceness. The problem is a lack of gospel. But wherever Jesus reigns by his truth, love reigns as "a mutual protection and kindness."[13] Paul was a man of courageous, apolitical independence. He was also a man of love, humility, and warmth:

> You were called to freedom, brothers. Only do not use your freedom as an opportunity for the flesh, but through love serve

13 Calvin, *Galatians*, 102.

one another. For the whole law is fulfilled in one word: "You shall love your neighbor as yourself." (Gal. 5:13–14)

Strong principles and humane relationships *together* mark a church as truly faithful to the gospel.

What, then, does it look like for a church to stand, rather than fall, by the gospel of justification by faith alone? It means that a church teaches the doctrine of grace-justification while that church also builds—and inevitably protects—a culture of grace-justification. In that kind of truly faithful church, no one is cornered or pressured to conform to a mere human demand. Everyone is freed to grow in grace, in gentle harmony with the other members. If confrontation is ever required, it is only "so that the truth of the gospel might be preserved for you" (Gal. 2:5). That cannot be a personal smackdown; it may only be the defense and confirmation of the gospel in both doctrine and culture.

For some churches, this larger understanding of gospel faithfulness might require repentance and reformation. We might not be as gospel-centered as we thought. Sadly, given human nature, nothing is easier for even a Protestant church than to enshrine the doctrines of Christ within a culture of ego. That is how we, in effect, de-gospel the gospel. And we end up dividing what the gospel unites. The gospel unites pastoral manliness with pastoral tenderness, and all other biblical polarities, as we see strikingly in Paul and perfectly in Jesus. How, then, with our destructive hearts, can we bear faithful witness to the gospel today? Is it even possible? Yes, if we will follow Paul's instruction: "But I say, walk by the Spirit, and you will not gratify the desires of the flesh" (Gal. 5:16).

Walking by the Spirit is not mechanical or formulaic. It's costly at a deeply personal level. But there is no other way. It means more than theological alertness. It means real-time dependence on God. It means putting ourselves under the judgment of his word. It means being forgiven constantly, making endless midcourse corrections, and following Christ with daily crucifixions of our pride.

In the flesh, we Bible-believing people shape our churches into doctrinally correct cultures of ugliness. But in the Spirit, and only in the Spirit, our churches become imperfect but visible proof of Jesus's truth and beauty. This is the faithfulness our generation must see.

Discussion Questions

1. As you read chapter 1, what was the one insight that stood out to you most, and why?

2. What could your church's culture more and more look like as the doctrine of justification by faith alone exerts its intended authority?

3. By God's grace, what new steps can your church take toward gospel doctrine creating gospel culture?

From Mere Knowledge to Shared Beauty

We don't believe what we've written in each chapter to be the final word, but we hope it will be the catalyst for constructive conversations in all our leadership teams and churches. So, at the end of each chapter, we've included a short dialogue between us that reflects the ongoing way we're working on these important themes. We hope you'll take these dialogues and continue them with your own teams and friends.

Sam: There can be a danger when we are rightly captivated by truth. As you found teaching through Romans, Ray, you want to get doctrine right? It matters. But particularly if you're predisposed to being a thinking type of person, it's easy for you to be focused there on getting doctrine right, getting your beliefs correct. It's easy, then, to have a natural blind spot to what it means to have an experience of what the doctrine is producing through you in the lives of other people.

Ray: For years, Sam, as a pastor, I didn't even realize that in emphasizing doctrine, I was feeding my pride. I don't think it's possible to be overly intellectual, but it is possible to be underrelational. The intellectual-only ministry sustained my preaching but only the preaching. In just bearing down on the correctness of the doctrine, I didn't realize how overbearing I was toward the people without realizing it.

Sam: I spent a few years doing campus ministry in Oxford with all these bright, young students. All of them had a huge capacity for thinking, reading, studying, and articulation. They wanted to be stretched, and they wanted to be fed. It was a wonderful context in which to teach. But the danger comes when you don't go beyond just teaching. There were things I wanted to get into a student's head. And once I'd gotten them into the student's head, I felt my job (and the student's job) was done. But while imparting knowledge is a glorious thing, it's woefully incomplete.

Ray: And it can even be a betrayal of the gospel. Because what exploded across the Mediterranean world in the first century was not brilliant ideas. What exploded and captivated the Roman Empire was a new kind of community, a new experience of community.

Sam: Yes, and that raises another dimension of what we're doing in this book: What is at stake in having gospel culture isn't just the internal health of a church, though that is crucial, but also our capacity to compel the world with it in our message of Jesus. It seems to me that, particularly in the cultural moment we now find ourselves, there's so much anger, polarization, and anxiety that relational beauty—more than any other time in my lifetime—will be so magnetic, so needed, so unusual, and so attractive to people who might not like what we believe but who find that kind of relational beauty hard to resist.

Open the Doors, Open Your Heart

A Culture of Gospel Welcome

Therefore welcome one another as Christ has welcomed you, for the glory of God.

ROMANS 15:7

THERE'S A SCENE in the political drama *The West Wing* where a new White House adviser disagrees with colleagues about an issue the administration is reviewing. A short time later, her opinion has become the new official policy, and it will be reflected in an address the president is soon to give. She's horrified. Words she'd said in passing now determined what would be broadcast from the Oval Office. One of her more experienced colleagues explains, "Well, we play with live ammo around here. It's a short day and a big country; we have to move fast."[1] An off-the-cuff conversation in the corridors of the White House becomes official policy and highly consequential for millions of people.

Sometimes the seemingly innocuous can be life changing. This can happen in a church too. The casual becomes consequential, with repercussions not only for the health of that church but also for its influence on the world.

For example, we might take the word *welcome* for granted. Such a common word doesn't strike us as filled with life-shaping significance. Maybe we associate it with a pastor's opening words at the start of a church service, words so taken for granted they're often not prepared. Or maybe we think of our initial contact with an unfamiliar face after the service, that awkward moment when we try to strike up a conversation. These moments of welcome—from the pastor and among the people—might feel peripheral to the *real* work of the church. They don't seem filled with potential.

But in fact, *welcome* is one of the most consequential words in our gospel vocabulary. Paul concludes two lengthy and profound chapters in his letter to the Romans that address church tensions by urging, of all things, welcome. In fact, the net impact of all of Paul's great theology in Romans comes down to this practical outcome: "Welcome one another as Christ has welcomed you, for the glory of God" (Rom. 15:7).

There it is. Welcome really does matter. The glory of God is bound up in it. We're called to welcome one another as Christ has welcomed us. There's the gospel in four words: "Christ has

---

1 *The West Wing*, season 2, episode 6, "The Lame Duck Congress," directed by Jeremy Kagan, aired November 8, 2000, on NBC.

welcomed us." Okay then, now we know how much welcome matters. When gospel doctrine starts to create gospel culture in a church, our mutual welcome comes alive!

Of course, a good-natured welcome is baked into the ground rules of any group or club. When I (Sam) was at college, I was involved in the university's student Thai Society, whose aim was to promote Thai culture within the university. (It was also an easy way for a broke student like me to regularly access cheap Thai food.) We'd meet once a month, and part of the agenda was looking for new people to draw into the group. It's how all groups work: we welcome people. But, as Ray has often said, the church isn't just meant to be a *new* community (there are plenty of those constantly springing up); it's meant to be a new *kind* of community. This entails a different *kind* of welcome—one that's ultimate origin isn't earth but heaven. We don't just welcome one another; we welcome one another *as Christ has welcomed us.*

Divine Welcome

The gospel, it turns out, is divine hospitality. We don't always think of it that way. We often think in more transactional terms: the gospel is *how* I'm made right with God, and faith in Christ's death is the hoop I must jump through to secure my place in heaven. But the gospel isn't simply God managing to problem solve our sin. It's God embracing us and welcoming us. The finished work of Christ on the cross is not God's way of saying to us, "You're free to go now" but "You're free to *come* now." He's not sending us off but inviting us in.

Another way to put this is that the gospel is both mercy and grace. Mercy is not getting what we deserve (in this case, God's judgment). Grace is getting what we don't deserve (in this case, adoption into God's family).

Many years passed before this distinction became apparent to me. Much of the preaching I had heard (and, I now shudder to think, delivered) focused on what we're saved *from*. Talks explained how Christ's death meant we no longer had to face hell and judgment. Now, this is obviously a weighty part of gospel preaching. Paul talks of being delivered "from the wrath to come" (1 Thess. 1:10). Elsewhere, concerning that future wrath, Paul writes about "that day when, according to my gospel, God judges the secrets of men by Christ Jesus" (Rom. 2:16).

For Paul, the second coming of Jesus to judge each one of us is "according to my gospel." In other words, the gospel *includes* the future judgment of humanity by Jesus. We must never drop this from our gospel preaching. It is vital.

But it isn't total. The gospel is also about what we're saved *for*. Which is where divine hospitality comes in. Jesus has not just *transacted* us out of our doom; he has brought us into his home. *Christ has welcomed you* is the gospel summed up super briefly.

We see this throughout the Bible. Consider just one Old Testament example:

> You shall treat the stranger who sojourns with you as the native among you, and you shall love him as yourself, for you were strangers in the land of Egypt: I am the LORD your God. (Lev. 19:34)

God was calling his people to do something radical: to treat the foreigner living in their land as though they were native. The outsider is to be treated as an insider. This was unheard of in the ancient world and goes against many cultural instincts today. But the rationale is clear: God's people had themselves been strangers. They'd been oppressed in Egypt because they were outsiders. And yet God had rescued them and brought them into a new land. He'd brought them in from the outside and given them a home within his land of promise. This was no incidental part of their national story. It was meant to define them and redefine how they would now treat others. What God had done for them they were now to do for others. God had welcomed them; they were to welcome the strangers around them. However radical it may seem compared with cultural norms then and now, it is obvious in the light of the welcome they and we have received from God. To fail to show hospitality to foreigners and outsiders would betray our identity and our history.

The New Testament also speaks of our salvation in these terms. Spiritually, we were distant and homeless:

Remember that you were at that time separated from Christ, alienated from the commonwealth of Israel and strangers to the covenants of promise, having no hope and without God in the world. But now in Christ Jesus you who once were far off have been brought near by the blood of Christ. (Eph. 2:12–13)

Look how dramatically God welcomed us in: We were far away from God; now we have been brought into his presence. We were strangers to God, oblivious to his grace; now we are part of his family, seated at his table. We see the same kind of before-and-after contrast in Romans:

Since, therefore, we have now been justified by his blood, much more shall we be saved by him from the wrath of God. For if while we were enemies we were reconciled to God by the death of his Son, much more, now that we are reconciled, shall we be saved by his life. (Rom. 5:9–10)

The difference is stunning: we deserved the wrath of God, but now we are fully justified; we were naturally enemies of God, but now we are fully reconciled to him. Paul is arguing from what God has already done to assure us of what God will yet do in completing our salvation. God has done the "hard" work of justifying and reconciling us, at no less a cost than the shedding of Christ's precious blood. We can be sure he'll do the remaining "easy" work of bringing us safely to journey's end in his presence above.

Paul puts it bluntly. We were not away from God in some unfortunate, neutral sense. We were *against* God. We were his enemies, determined to keep our distance. Yet look where we are. We're now brothers of Jesus, seated around the Father's table as full, permanent members of his household. That's divine hospitality for sure!

So, when Paul asks us to welcome one another as Christ has welcomed us, he's not asking us to do something easy. Christ's welcome was anything but easy. It wasn't a wink and a smile as he passed by. He came to us when we were far from him. He bled for us, laying down his life in humble service. He welcomed us by experiencing divine unwelcome himself, being forsaken by God (Matt. 27:46). He brought us in by being thrust out himself, suffering outside the city gate (Heb. 13:12). We've been included because he was excluded. He welcomed us at the cost of all he had. He held nothing back. His welcome is no small matter. No true welcome ever is.

This welcome of Christ can and should so captivate us that it changes how we "do church." This welcome of Christ can and should grip our hearts and pour out of us to one another. We're to behold his welcome in such a way that sharing it with one another is inevitable and beautiful.

We pastors are to be a key part of that.

Welcome as Christ Has Welcomed You

One of the most overlooked qualifications for a pastor is that he be hospitable (1 Tim. 3:2). I've been interviewed for the role of a pastor a few times over the years, but I've never been asked about the priority of hospitality in my lifestyle. We can see why. A prospective pastor's vision, preaching gifts, godliness, and leadership style all feel weightier. We just assume they're hospitable, by which we typically mean they're good at occasionally having people around for dinner.

But Paul has a different view of hospitality: a pastor "must be above reproach, the husband of one wife, sober-minded, self-controlled, respectable, hospitable" (1 Tim. 3:2). Amazingly, hospitality shares top billing with marital faithfulness and being above reproach. Christian leadership requires Christian hospitality. Given how welcome-shaped the gospel is, this should now not surprise us. The pastor's own life should reflect this, as should his words every Sunday in church.

Let's think about those opening moments of a church service. They couldn't be more important. They're the storefront window of Christ's welcome for people who walk into church feeling like outsiders—which is nearly everyone every Sunday.

Paul didn't write, "Welcome one another as people at the fitness club down the road welcome each other." We're not meant to be conveying *our* welcome but *Christ's* welcome. It is not about exchanging a cultural pleasantry but declaring a heavenly reality. We're meant to be inviting brokenhearted sinners to collapse into the open arms of Jesus.

The start of our gathered worship is possibly the most precious moment in the whole service. We have only a minute to make it a *gospel* moment. But, with God's help, we want to rearrange people's spiritual reality right from the get-go. We want to lead them from

I don't know why I came this week.
This isn't for me.
I'm just no good at Christianity.
No one here gets me.
How long will I be stuck here?

to

You mean Jesus is really like this?
I'm so relieved I came.
I so need this.
Maybe there is hope for me.
I can't wait to come back next Sunday.

It's hard to overstate the importance of the welcome at the start of the service, and how much is lost when it is not handled carefully, pastorally, gospely.

I mentioned in the previous chapter a long-term member of a previous church of mine who had been absent for a few weeks while things were messy in her life. She'd come to believe that there was a baseline level of acceptability she needed to reach to come to church, and we weren't going to see her until she'd got herself back up to that level. Bear in mind this lady had been receiving sound evangelical ministry for *years*. I am confident she'd be able to articulate the gospel clearly. But there was a profound disconnect between the gospel that had been repeatedly preached to her and that, on one level, she understood perfectly well, and what she *really* believed in the depths of her heart at that moment. She's not alone in experiencing this disconnect. It's amazing how many of us instinctively think this way. It's as if the Christian life is a video game where you must progress to a certain point to unlock the "church going" level.

Another time I'd suggested to our congregation's lay leadership team that we might offer prayer ministry after the service for any who desired it. One of our key leaders immediately said she'd never want to go forward for prayer herself because she wouldn't want anyone to see that she might have a problem. Again, she'd been at solid Bible-believing churches for decades. But her comment revealed that, at a deep level, she experienced church as a place where she had to have her life together.

The welcome on a Sunday morning is where we pastors deconstruct the posing of nongospel culture and reconstruct in its place the beauty of gospel culture. The opening moments of our services are when we can establish new gospel ground rules for why and how we gather as Christians. We're not here to do God a favor, to give him some company for an hour or so, to make him feel better. We're not here to pay a weekly religion tax so that he gets off our back for the next six days. We're not here to get our respectability card stamped for another week. We're here for just one reason: Christ has welcomed us. We need to wrap our brains around that good news. We need to hit refresh on that surprising reality every single Sunday.

Someone might think that we don't necessarily need to make the gospel *the* issue at the welcome, when there are songs, prayers, sacraments, and a sermon that will declare the gospel. Surely, we can trust the rest of the service to bring home the reality of grace and not put so much weight on the welcome at the start.

Ocean liners are famously hard to turn around. Their bulk and weight make it tricky to maneuver, so it matters to set the course correctly. Once the journey is underway, it is difficult to change direction. Similarly, the opening welcome sets the tone for everything else. It establishes the culture of the whole service—something that's hard to change once the ministry is up and running.

And there's an even more urgent reason why the welcome is consequential: How could we bear making anyone wait before experiencing the welcome of Jesus? It isn't a formality. His gracious welcome is the whole point.

I've found over the years that it can sometimes take most of the service for people to get to where they start to believe God might truly love them. Perhaps by the end of the sermon. Perhaps in time to enjoy the final song. But what if, with God's help, we usher the people into this gospel glory right at the start? What if, instead of them slowly warming up over the course of an hour or so, they start out experiencing Christ's welcome? Then, for the rest of the service, they can bask in it! I'm writing this amid a European heat wave, on vacation in a musty old building that has never heard of air conditioning. My only way to cope has been to periodically slip into the pool to cool myself down. The tingle of refreshing, cool water on a hot, sticky body is utterly blissful. I find myself lingering there, marveling at how good it feels.

That's what a church, refreshed with gospel culture, feels like to exhausted sinners. They aren't standing by the side of the pool, being told how cool it is, and only after a while getting in. But from the first moment of the service, they are welcomed in. The pastor gently, sincerely declares the refreshing grace of Jesus. And he washes it over their weary souls through the call to worship from the outset of the service.

This is an area where I've changed as a pastor. I used to think I was welcoming people to church. Romans 15:7 has made me realize I'm welcoming people to *Christ*. I'm not trying to break the cultural ice; I'm aiming for *spiritual renewal right then and there*. I'm longing for the welcome of Jesus to be a felt reality from the opening seconds of the service.

There are many ways to provide such a gospel welcome. Each church will rightly have its own traditions, personality, denominational responsibilities, and so on. This isn't about being a little more Baptist here or Anglican there. It's about establishing clearly, from the first moment the pastor steps up in front of the congregation, that this isn't like any other gathering around the city. Our meeting does not revolve around a shared interest, common cause, or cultural expectation. We are here in church because Jesus's heart-melting welcome has pulled us in. Where else would we be?

The pastoral welcome is not the only time and place where we want the welcome of Jesus to be unmissable, of course. After all, Paul's command to "welcome one another as Christ has welcomed you" applies to more than the pastor and more than a church service. But wouldn't it be wonderful if our pastoral welcome Sunday by Sunday became the jump start for our week-long intention to make the welcome of Jesus less theoretical and more personal? Having received the welcome of Christ in church, it becomes a lot easier to share the welcome of Christ all week long. In our angry world, may his welcome go viral!

Jesus's Welcome in Real Time

Let's look at Jesus's welcome in action by examining his interactions with two different but desperately needy people in the New Testament. One is a woman, the other a man. One is a despised Samaritan, the other a Jewish leper. One is excluded because of her behavior, the other because of a condition he cannot change. Both were despised. Both were shunned. Significantly, both are nameless. But both are welcomed by Jesus.

When Jesus encountered the Samaritan woman in John 4, she was there at the well at the time of day most ideally suited for avoiding others (4:6). She was an outcast. Her story was a tragedy of five failed marriages. She was the kind of woman mothers want their sons to avoid. Yet Jesus initiated a conversation with her (4:7). He approached her and dignified her. Later, as our Lord's welcome was reaching still others, he told his disciples something extraordinary. His ministry of finding and restoring brokenhearted sinners wasn't a mere duty. To him, it was a satisfying feast: "My food is to do the will of him who sent me and to accomplish his work" (4:34). Jesus is not reaching out to this woman and her community because some technicality obligates him to. He *loves* getting close to outsiders.

Consider the time a leper did the unthinkable by coming up to Jesus in Mark 1. Leprosy was highly infectious, incurable, and thought to be spiritually defiling. As a result, lepers were excluded from the community. A leper even poking his head around someone's door would be enough to contaminate the entire household. Physical contact with a leper was like touching a corpse. Physically and socially, leprosy located its victims far outside acceptable society. For a leper to come up to Jesus in this way was shocking. It would be worse than a highly infectious Covid sufferer coughing and spluttering in the face of a healthy person.

This man was toxic, bringing only contamination and defilement. He was too radioactive to get close to anyone. But somehow, this ultimate refugee heard that Jesus *wasn't* just anyone. He's aware of something surprising about Jesus: he can heal and restore. The man's leprosy was a living death, and yet Jesus can raise the dead to new life. This man also recognizes something about himself—not just his condition, but his unworthiness: "*If you will*, you can make me clean" (1:40). He believes Jesus *can* but doesn't presume that Jesus *should*. Healing is not something this man can claim as his right. He is at the mercy of Jesus, who owes him nothing except perhaps a scolding for being there in the first place.

Ordinarily, this leper would have been sharply rebuked for this behavior. But however unthinkable his actions are, they are no more unthinkable than what Jesus does next: "Moved with pity, he stretched out his hand and touched him and said to him, 'I will; be clean'" (1:41). Jesus is moved with pity. Not revulsion. Not disgust. Not even indifference. He is indignant, not at the man for his actions but for what the leprosy has done to him. He doesn't recoil and withdraw. He's moved by this man, toward this man.

Mark tells us not only how Jesus felt but also what he did. Astonishingly, he reaches out and *touches* the man. It would likely have been years since anyone had touched the dear man. No hug, no arm around the shoulder, not even a fist bump—for all those long years. Physical contact with a leper was life-threatening. No surprise, then, that the Old Testament law insisted that lepers remain isolated, far from everyone else.

But Jesus *isn't* everyone else. He not only touches this man but says to him, "I will; be clean" (1:41). His pity springs into action by touching and healing this man. Mark wants us to be in no doubt: "And immediately the leprosy left him" (1:42). Touching a leprous man was dangerous—but, in this case it is dangerous to the leprosy rather than to Jesus. Jesus's cleanness is far more contagious than the leper's uncleanness.

Let's just pause right there. Whatever darkness inside of you troubles your heart, whatever capacities for wickedness and stupidity lurk within, whatever still haunts you from your past, however fearful you are that you will never change, know this: *your sin does not intimidate Jesus*. What is right in him far outweighs what is wrong in you. There is more grace in him than guilt in you. He is better at saving than you are at sinning. It is at the point where all of us feel the most disgusted with ourselves, the most hopeless and most worthy of judgment—it is in our worst defilement that we find Jesus the most tender and gracious toward us.

This is Christ's welcome. He moves toward the needy, the outcast, the messed-up, the sinful. He doesn't recoil in disgust. He doesn't keep his distance. He makes the first move, he approaches, he is moved, he reaches out, he heals and restores. This is what it means for Christ to welcome us. This is what we're to offer one another. It's meant to go viral! Our churches, by believing the gospel, can become ground zero for the welcome of Jesus in our cities and communities.

Sharing Jesus's Welcome with One Another

The welcome of Jesus can translate into our openness to one another in our churches and to strangers outside:

> Do not be slothful in zeal, be fervent in spirit, serve the Lord. Rejoice in hope, be patient in tribulation, be constant in prayer. Contribute to the needs of the saints and seek to show hospitality. (Rom. 12:11–13)

What might surprise us here is not that hospitality is commanded but where this command is found. Paul puts it up there with prayer and serving the poor, with persevering in times of difficulty and with being spiritually fervent. Hospitality is *that* important. But no wonder, given how the gospel itself declares an extraordinary act of hospitality.

Given this context, these seemingly disparate commands must be more deeply interconnected than we realize. The Christian life is an integrated whole. Our various obligations in Christ are like an ecosystem. We can't neglect one area and expect the others to flourish. So how could we maintain a flourishing prayer life or cheerful generosity to the poor or a heart burning with affection for Christ if we're neglecting hospitality?

In this sense, showing hospitality is not only for the sake of others but also for us. *We* will start to suffer as total human beings if we neglect it. Welcoming others reenacts the gospel itself, especially as we open our homes and hearts to those we might not even know. It deepens our own openness to Christ. Welcoming others can reinternalize the welcome of Christ to us.

For this reason, Paul tells us not only to show hospitality but to *seek* to show it. We're on the hunt. We're keeping our eyes peeled. We're sitting on the edge of our seats, eager for opportunities to welcome others as Christ has welcomed us. Our own faith will weaken if we don't practice hospitality.

Likewise, Peter urges us to "show hospitality to one another *without grumbling*" (1 Pet. 4:9). Merely performing the task while resenting it in our hearts shows that we're calloused to the gospel. My wonder at the welcome of Christ is diminished if I find myself unenthusiastic to give others a taste of it. Sulky hospitality is no hospitality at all. If we don't enjoy offering it, who would enjoy receiving it?

So, what are we being called to do?

Let's identify the cultural blind spots that keep us from understanding what hospitality involves. In much of the Western world, hospitality is performative. It's about proving how well we can cook or giving a tour of our beautiful home. It's showing off an Instagram version of our lives. (No wonder we call it *entertaining*.) Biblical hospitality, however, is about opening up to others rather than trying to impress them. This means all of us can be great at hospitality. It takes only humble willingness.

Who cares if we don't have a fancy home with which to wow others? Friends of mine in New York City live in apartments so small I can stand in the middle and touch all four walls, so they do much of their hospitality outside the home rather than inside. They go out for coffee, walk in the park, or run errands. For them, hospitality is about doing real life together. You don't need a big home. You just need a big heart, like the heart of Christ toward *you*.

We can even be hospitable when we're busy. It's not about adding yet another activity to an already overcrowded schedule; it's about taking what we're already doing and involving other people—letting them into our crazy lives and together discovering the Lord's kindness right there. I know people who get together to do laundry! A friend and I went through a time of always getting our hair cut together until I moved to a different part of the city. Another friend and I often go to the supermarket together. Impressive? No. Doable, and graced with the welcome of Christ himself? Yes!

It might feel as though we've strayed a bit from the welcome of Christ, but, in fact, we have pressed in further. "Welcoming one another" embodies and declares what Christ has done for us. Heaven's welcome becomes real in our own. We have a wonderful opportunity, every single week, to reflect the heart of God; for his welcome to radiate out among us, and into the world beyond.

Discussion Questions

1. As you read chapter 2, what was the one insight that stood out to you most, and why?

2. In what ways does the welcome of Christ (Rom. 15:7) dignify and expand our understandings of a friendly welcome at church?

3. What patterns in your church inadvertently diminish the welcoming power of the gospel, and how can your church get free of those personal or traditional hindrances?

Open Wide the Doors

Ray: Many people walk into church expecting to get a pep talk or maybe even a tongue-lashing. But exhausted, weary, defeated sinners don't need a cheerleading experience from the front.

Sam: They don't need scolding.

Ray: I strongly agree. The first two minutes of the service really matter. That's when the pastor sets the tone for the rest of the service. The welcome is pastoral ministry. It's not something you hand off to whoever's leading the band or the singing, whatever it may be. I don't remember what the occasion was, but I discovered a call to worship on the home page of the website of Tenth Presbyterian Church in Philadelphia. I don't know if they composed it themselves or if it came out of the Presbyterian tradition, but I was captivated by it. Here's what it said:

> To all who are weary and need rest, to all who mourn and long for comfort, to all who fail and desire strength, to all who sin and need a Savior: this church opens wide her doors with a welcome from Jesus, the friend of sinners.

That's what I want to say to Nashville. That's what I want to say to the world because who isn't exhausted these days and in need of rest? By the way, in a Bible Belt place like Nashville, people walk into church expecting that the message they're going to get from the pastor that day is, "Y'all are slackers. Y'all need to re-up. Y'all need to get serious this time," and so forth.

But Romans 15:7 says, "Therefore welcome one another as Christ has welcomed you, for the glory of God." Where can the glory of God be seen in the world today beyond the Grand Canyon and the Isle of Skye? In our churches! The glory of God is seen in our welcome.

Sam: And Paul's not just saying, "Hey guys, please be nice." He's telling us that our gospel doctrine creates a gospel culture, a new way of welcoming. There's something distinctive about the welcome we have for each other because it's meant to be of the same species of welcome as the one Christ has shown us.

Come into the Light

A Culture of Gospel Honesty

*But if we walk in the light, as he is in the light,
we have fellowship with one another, and the
blood of Jesus his Son cleanses us from all sin.*

1 JOHN 1:7

YOUR CHURCH CAN BE not only the most honest church in town but the most honest *anything* in town—more honest than any bar. I (Ray) love the story from Donald Miller's book *Blue Like Jazz*, when the Christian students on that Oregon college campus wondered how to respond to the annual week-long drunken orgy and asked, "What do we do?" They built a confessional, like in a Roman Catholic church, right at the center of campus. And instead of inviting the non-Christian students to come confess their sins to the Christians, they invited everyone to come hear the Christian students confess *their* sins. A student would come in, and a believer would tell all.[1]

How humbly prophetic! The Christians weren't denouncing others' sins but admitting their own. And what a relief it is to get real!

Nothing is uglier than a church posing and pretending. A dishonest church denies the gospel by the church's reality, even if it professes the gospel in its theory. But nothing is more beautiful than a church walking together in the light.

Have you ever seen a church with too much tenderness, humility, and willingness to own up? No! So why doesn't every church embrace a culture of gospel honesty? Why doesn't yours? Jesus is right there, waiting for his true followers to stumble together out from the darkness into his light. Every church can be living proof of the gospel by embodying a culture of honesty—honesty about God in his grace, and honesty about us in our mess.

Stumbling toward Beauty

We're not saying honesty is easy. In our world, including our church world, the grace of Jesus is so radical it baffles our deepest intuitions. His mercy for the undeserving makes the gospel hard to accept at conversion and hard to hold onto along the way. We deeply fear Jesus can't stomach the real, behind-the-scenes, unrehabilitated us. We expect (and suspect) that he despises us, that he *should* despise us. But the gospel insists he loves, forgives, justifies, adopts, and rejoices over us and that he will never stop,

1   Donald Miller, *Blue Like Jazz: Nonreligious Thoughts on Christian Spirituality* (Nashville: Thomas Nelson, 2003), chap. 11.

no matter what mess we bring out into his light. Whenever we dare believe his gospel, that's when we find ourselves walking in the light. That's real Christianity, and it's beautiful.

Are we all clear on what our churches are primarily for? Every church is for enjoying who Jesus is. *He* is our all (Eph. 1:22–23). Everything else in life, not just in church but in all human life, flows from him. Let's not *assume* we see him clearly. Let's *examine* whether we see him clearly, especially his counterintuitive grace.

Our primary task as pastors in our generation is not to *preserve* the original Christianity Jesus created. Our task is to *recover* his original Christianity. We can go back. We can peel away the artificial layers of "church" and go back to basics. We can shed every bit of hand-me-down, derivative, hybrid Christianity that rubbed off on us somehow but has never helped us. Let's together, in our time, rediscover the true Christianity Jesus himself looks at and says, "That's what *I'm* talking about!" Let's get free of secondhand substitutes and go find out what the grace of Jesus can do for inexcusable people like us.

Have you seen a church anywhere with too much forgiveness, too much freedom from the past, too much hope and joy? Gospel doctrine creates a gospel culture where those beautiful realities come down, and it feels like heaven on earth! Why not *your* church? Why not *now*? What are we waiting for? There's not a better Jesus or a better gospel. So why not say to your church this Sunday, "Friends, we're just stumbling forward together, finding out how good Jesus really is. It can only get better. Let's not hold back. Let's keep going."?

A great next step opens for any church at 1 John 1:7. Here's the beautiful culture of gospel honesty in one verse: "But if we walk in the light, as he is in the light, we have fellowship with one another, and the blood of Jesus his Son cleanses us from all sin."

Let's think it through.

God Is Light

The context is 1 John 1:5: "This is the message we have heard from him and proclaim to you, that God is light, and in him is no darkness at all." The "we" there is the original eyewitnesses of Jesus. They were with him for three years. Can you imagine hanging out with Jesus for three years? What if we had one thousand lunches with Jesus to listen to him and talk with him? *They did.*

John is saying that we can have that same Jesus today. In fact, we *must* have the real, original Jesus. John wrote against *heresy* (specifically the heresy that Christ was not fully human). It had already entered the young Christian church, in just the second generation. He tells his readers that spiritual integrity *demands* going back to apostolic orthodoxy. The same is true for us today. Our historic distance from those times can neither rescue us from this heresy nor block out the light of God. This heresy is with us today; but so is the light, and he's still shining brightly. We too can walk in his light. We today can experience real, original Christianity. We *must* experience it. That is John's point.

But do you see how John helps us get there? He sums up, in 1:5, the basic message of Jesus. Our Lord said many things. But when his original followers boil it down, how do they summarize Jesus's message? John says, "God is light, and in him is no darkness at all." Eleven words. Just forty-five characters, plus a comma and a period. It's not even a full tweet.

But the message of Jesus can be distilled to that foundational truth—though the implications are endless. And obviously, Jesus did not come to tell us how wonderful we are. But he did come to tell us how beautiful God is. "God is light, and in him is no darkness at all."

Have you ever seen ugly light? Dirty light? Dishonest light? What the light reveals may unsettle us. But what problems do we discover in the light itself? Is there anything about the light we must worry about, apologize for, or filter out? The point is obvious. Jesus came into this world, briefly but eloquently, revealing God to us. His message was that God is the only one in the universe whom we can welcome and open up to with zero caution. God will never lie to us, never betray our trust, never twist reality to our disadvantage.

The deepest reason for all our personal problems, and all the evils of history, is that we don't know how beautiful God is. We barricade ourselves against the one we can most eagerly receive. Without him, all we're left with is ourselves. Reynolds Price, the brilliant skeptic, showed us where we then end up: "There is no Creator and there never was. The universe is pure unillumined matter, where senseless atoms and vicious creatures stage the awful pageants of their wills."[2] That is the world we've created from the messages inside our heads. Jesus came to us with another message entirely: "God is light, and in him is no darkness at all." To Jesus, that conviction wasn't a sidebar. It's what his whole life stood for.

No Darkness in Him At All

Do our churches accept this vision of God? Have we wrestled with and thought through the reality that God is light? Are we

---

2 Reynolds Price, *Letter to a Man in the Fire: Does God Exist and Does He Care?* (1999; repr., New York: Touchstone, 2000), 54.

tracking with Jesus, or are we using him as the champion of our own self-invented messages?

Facing God can be a terrifying prospect. The Bible says no man can see God and live (Ex. 33:20). If we saw God in his industrial-strength glory right now, we would disintegrate. We may think, "But of course. How could it be otherwise? God is so fierce and menacing!" But the truth is the opposite. The reason we can't experience direct exposure to God is that we couldn't handle the intense happiness, the ravishing beauty, the nuclear-powered glory of who God really is.

Psalm 27:4, in the old translation preserved in the Book of Common Prayer, looks forward to that day when we'll be able to behold "the fair beauty of the Lord."[3] Jonathan Edwards uses a fun word to help us think of God more accurately: "It is a thing truly happifying to the soul of man to see God."[4] To see God is *happifying*! That's who God really is. Jesus came to let us in on God's happifying light. And every other light, every other happiness and beauty, contains at least some elements of darkness. Other happinesses will let us down, maybe even break our hearts. But there's zero darkness in God.

God's Light Produces Honest Culture

The beauty we long for in our churches starts with the clarity Jesus gave us in our doctrine of God. And what John is urging upon us here is not a denominational option, where we are free to take differing positions on secondary and tertiary doctrines. The

---

3   Anglican Church in North America, *The Book of Common Prayer* (Huntington Beach: Anglican Liturgy Press, 2019), 299.

4   Jonathan Edwards, "The Pure in Heart Blessed" (1753), Bible Bulletin Board (website), accessed December 19, 2022, https://www.biblebb.com.

apostle is calling us back to basic Christianity, starting with our view of God himself. How, then, *do* you perceive God? Where did you even get your idea of him? If your view of God is true to original, Jesus-given Christianity, here's one way you'll know: not by taking a true-false exam on paper but by noticing your relationships with other Christians. When we start seeing God the way Jesus did, we're so struck by his beauty that we feel both humbled and safe—that is, we're finally free to face ourselves without fear of condemnation. All our aloofness, both from fear and pride, weakens in the light of who God really is.

If it's gospel culture we want in our churches—and we do—then we won't get traction simply by trying harder to be nice. The remedy is more profound. We will get traction for gospel culture by perceiving God with gospel eyes, the eyes of Jesus. Gospel culture isn't a glaze of superficial smiley niceness on the surface of deep and robust Christianity.[5] No, gospel culture is itself deep and robust Christianity. Anything less is shallow, including theologically serious but relationally oblivious Christianity.

One essential to real Christianity remaining vital in our generation is not in how we behave but in *how we see God.* This was the great burden both on Jesus's and the apostle John's heart. It's now the burden on our heart. Our Lord and the apostles were willing to *suffer* to help us come alive to the beauty of God. This heavenly vision is the message at the center of real, original, apostolic, universal, time-tested, nonweird, beautiful Christianity.

Think about it in terms of the geography of J. R. R. Tolkien's *Lord of the Rings.* We don't see Christ's reflection in Mordor. We see

---

5   Ray Ortlund and T. J. Tims, "Ground-Level Gospel Culture," *You're Not Crazy* (podcast), The Gospel Coalition (website), July 7, 2022, https://www.thegospelcoalition.org/.

his reflection in the Shire. Mordor is where all the worldly power is, but the Shire is where the human beauty is. In the new world Christ is creating, the beauty of gentle humaneness will always be more captivating than the power of worldly demandingness. Look at Jesus himself. We feel both humbled and safe with him. We can relax, calm down, open up, and tell him *everything*. Our darkness cannot extinguish his light. His cross and resurrection prove that.

Walking in the Light[6]

That insight is how gospel doctrine creates gospel culture. Other people begin to realize they are safe around us. Their lives are even a little more beautiful because of us—because we put them above ourselves. But what does this look like practically? In 1 John 1:7, the apostle explains how we can walk together in the light of who God is, and never stop. Let's take it one phrase at a time.

"But if we walk in the light . . ." We don't have to run. We just walk together, one step at a time. Obviously, we can't sit around passively. But we can be defiant. We can dare to believe that God is light, so that we *refuse* to stay stuck, recycling the same old, same old, blah, defunct "church" routine that isn't breathing life into us or anyone else. Creative innovation *can* help, at a practical level, to crack our hearts open to God's newness of life.[7]

What, then, does it mean for us to "walk in the light"? It cannot mean living in sinless perfection. After all, the light is where we

---

6 Portions of this section are adapted from Ray Ortlund, "Walking in the Light, Part 1" Renewal Ministries, August 7, 2011, https://renewalministries.com/.

7 Timothy Keller, "Revival: Ways and Means," *Timothy Keller* (blog), January 10, 2011, https://timothykeller.com/.

find *cleansing* from sin. The context in 1:5–10, clearly, is all about facing ourselves and our sins honestly. So, *walking in the light is opening up to an honest relationship with Jesus and one another, so we're free to grow.* If God really is light with no darkness at all, if God really is beauty with nothing distasteful at all, then we really can come out of hiding. We can get real with him. We can get real with one another. We don't have to appear better than we really are.

So, we can stop making excuses: "But Lord, this is my personality." "But Lord, look what my wife did." "But Lord, you can't expect me actually to *obey* the Bible." That's not walking in the light. It's hanging back in the shadows of evasion and denial, and it's unfair to him and injurious to us. Paul Tournier, the brilliant Swiss psychiatrist, wrote, "A diffuse and vague guilt feeling kills the personality, whereas the conviction of sin gives life to it."[8]

It's so freeing to come right out with it, call sin "sin," and bring it to Jesus, because he puts it under his own blood, and then it's gone forever. His cross opened the door for us to enter an honest relationship with him and one another, relationships where we can finally relax, breathe, rethink, and start changing. "Walking in the light" means gentle honesty about what isn't working in our lives, about how we're not doing well, about our sins and failures, about our regrets and fears. It's bringing our mess to the Lord and laying it down before him and one another with transparency. That's walking in the light.

"*. . . as he is in the light . . .*" God is light. And now we see something else: God is also *in* the light. Why does John say that? He wants to emphasize that God isn't hiding from us. He isn't

8 Paul Tournier, *Escape from Loneliness*, trans. John S. Gilmour (Philadelphia: Westminster, 1962), 163.

playing "Catch me if you can." God stands right out in the obvious place of truth, honesty, and reality, right where we can find him and be helped by him. So, what on earth are we doing anywhere else? "Church" can be an ideal place to hide from God. But when a church turns toward gospel culture, it's also the best place to find God. Now is the best time to get fed up enough with empty unreality, so that we start admitting it. Here's a sentence from Francis Schaeffer I can't escape:

> As I travel about and speak in many countries, I am impressed with the number of times I am asked by Christians about the loss of reality in their Christian lives.[9]

That can change. We can get back to personal reality with the living God, the way we experienced it as new Christians. We don't get there by changing churches but by leaving self-concealment and entering honest self-disclosure together. Whenever we're no longer experiencing reality with God, we should bluntly ask ourselves whether we're clinging to an unreal and self-invented construct of ourselves. What hope is there for experiencing reality when our false selves make God as unreal to us as we make ourselves to others? Why not just come clean? Then we can come together again as a band of ragtag sinners who flat-out believe the gospel enough to step right out into the light, *where God himself is waiting for us* with his arms open wide!

When we walk in the light as he is in the light, we are renewed in our experience of two great realities. Here's the first:

---

9 Francis Schaeffer, *True Spirituality* (Wheaton, IL: Tyndale House, 1971), 60.

"*. . . we have fellowship with one another . . .*" We all know what it's like to be at a dinner party on a Saturday night where everyone is friendly, the food is great, and the laughter is hilarious. Then it gets even better. How? One courageous individual sitting at the table gets real. He or she starts admitting what's really going on in life—what's hard, how he or she is struggling with loneliness, failure, fear, sadness, doubt, and sin. Suddenly the atmosphere in the room changes. It gets quiet. Everyone leans in and becomes more attentive. A tender sense is felt by all, that we really are among friends. Everyone knows it's a safe place. *That* is "fellowship."

Hopefully that reality is also felt in the fellowship hall at church, but it can happen anywhere. It happens whenever we sinners so believe the gospel that we let our guard down and let others in. Then everyone begins to discover how much they have in common. That glorious solidarity is "fellowship with one another."

This fellowship between real sinners in the light of the real God is uniquely Christian. You don't need me to point out that the world isn't like this, except occasionally as a lingering echo of Christianity. The world is harsh. No one ever measures up. No one ever owns up. Everyone keeps faking it. Again, Paul Tournier wisely wrote,

> In everyday life we are continually soaked in this unhealthy atmosphere of mutual criticism, so much so that we are not always aware of it and we find ourselves drawn unwittingly into an implacable vicious circle: every reproach evokes a feeling of guilt in the critic as much as in the one criticized, and each

one gains relief from his guilt in any way he can, by criticizing other people and in self-justification.[10]

No one enjoys being judged. But it happens every day through the comparisons implicit in advertising, the winners and losers in politics, and so forth. We're swimming daily through an ocean of mercilessness. How do we cope with that? One way is to off-load our resentment about being judged by judging others. If merciless judgments are the path we choose, we'll spiral down into endless mutual attacks, sometimes verbal, usually mental. No wonder our world, even our churches, careen from conflict to conflict!

But the cross of Jesus breaks that vicious cycle. It creates a new culture of fellowship, belonging, intimacy, understanding, sympathy, and solidarity. How? Jesus took our real moral guilt onto himself—not only our own false accusations of others but also God's just judgment against the sins we are too afraid to face. Jesus didn't just salve our guilty anxieties, though he cares about them too. In his radical grace, Jesus laid his axe at the root of our fearful isolation when at the cross he absorbed God's wrath against us and then gave to us nothing but love.

Now we share his radical grace together. That's what it means to be a healthy church. That's the makings of gospel culture. We stand in the light of his holiness and grace together with a safety this world can't offer. We have many sins in common, but we also have a gracious Savior in common. And as we believe this good news and act upon it with personal honesty, admitting the truth

10 Paul Tournier, *Guilt and Grace* (New York: Harper and Brothers, 1962), 15–16.

about ourselves, sympathy flows back and forth among us with powerful beauty.

"... *and the blood of Jesus his Son cleanses us from all sin.*" The second reality that awaits us when we walk together in honesty before the Lord is cleansing. A church is more than a mere human support group. The empathy we share is wonderful, but more importantly, a church is where a *miracle* happens. The sacred blood of Jesus comes down on sinners with cleansing power, felt power, as the cross of two thousand years ago washes into our needs today. How does this take place? When we stop posing, and when we bring our real shortcomings, betrayals, and failures to Christ in fellowship with one another. That is when he meets us by his Spirit with fresh cleansing.

There's *no sin* that his blood cannot cleanse away. The text says, "*all* sin." So, think of your worst. It's hard, I know, but think of the sin you most regret, the sin in your past that haunts and troubles you to this day. *That* is the point in your existence where Jesus loves you the most tenderly. That is the sin Jesus bled to cleanse away from you. Your renewal means that much to him. So, take a step out into the light, then another step, then another. Confess your sin to the Lord and to a trusted friend who will pray for you (James 5:16). Don't avoid it anymore. Face it. Admit it. Speak it. Begin a new lifestyle of honest confession. Don't hold back. Jesus won't hold back either.

You will start to feel clean again because Jesus bore *every* sin you cannot bear. Honor Jesus and his finished work on the cross by your open honesty because that wretched, intimidating sin doesn't define or own you anymore. That sin has no right to you. It does not deserve to rob you of the fellowship and cleansing you long for. You, a sinner, a desperate sinner, have been redefined by Jesus's blood that gushed out for you. And as you and your friends at church experience this together, more and more you'll be living proof that real, original, Jesus-given, apostolic Christianity is alive and well in the world today.

Pastor, real Christianity is your only legitimate ministry. Jesus started something new two thousand years ago, and it's your inheritance today. He told us about God to bring us together at our real points of need. Don't settle for less than gospel doctrine creating honest gospel culture at your church. Embrace it. Enjoy it. Spread it. There will be no end to the Lord's blessing on you and through you.

Discussion Questions

1. As you read chapter 3, what was the one insight that stood out to you most, and why?

2. In view of 1 John 1:7, James 5:16, and other Bible passages, it seems odd we Christians and our churches rarely confess wrongs, apologize, and, if possible, repair broken relationships. Why? What holds us back from gospel honesty?

3. How might your church contribute to a growing culture of honesty, confession, and owning up among Christians in our generation?

Conversation about Confession

Ray: Sam, I'm now seventy-three years old. One of the most important things right now in my existence is preparing to die well. I don't want you and my family and Immanuel Church and Renewal Ministries to have to clean up a mess I'd left concealed after I die. I want to die honorably so y'all can weep at my funeral and rejoice and move on, so my memory provides a lingering blessing into the next generation. The only way I know to end well is to live well, which is not sinlessness, but in the confession of sin. Pastors who have no one to whom they confess their sins are on their way to trouble.

James says, "Confess your sins to one another and pray for one another, that you may be healed" (5:16). He doesn't say to shame, embarrass, corner, or pressure one another. Sam, I don't even like the category "accountability" because I've seen it used in a way that's bossy and coercive and shaming. The text says to pray for one another, not fix one another. It doesn't even say advise one another, though there's a place for that. But "pray for one another, that you may be healed."

Sam: Someone asked me once, "How do you—out of the countless number of sins in your life—know which to confess to your friends?" I said, "For me, it's quite easy. As I'm driving over on a Monday afternoon to see you guys, it's the thing I don't want to share with you." That's normally the clue as to what I need to confess. I just ask, "What don't I want them to know about from this past week?"

Ray: Yes. I believe that in a gospel culture, sinful people (which is all of us) find safety where we can open up with one another and admit to what's going on and gently pray for one another. That can only end well because the Bible says God promises healing in that place. We pastors need healing. If we pastors will go there, if we'll just say, "Okay, I'm done with my isolation. I'm done with my aloofness. For by God's grace and for his glory, I'm going to find that place of healing. I'm going to find one or two other men in my city and meet with them regularly to tell them my mess and pray together."

Sam: That's part of welcoming one another as Christ has welcomed us, isn't it? I mean, one of the freeing things the gospel gives us is the truth that God knows the worst about us, and it's still safe to come to him. When we see that translated into our relationships, they become safe. Then it's safe for me to let you know some of the worst things about me, and doing so reinforces the truth of the gospel.

Ray: I wonder whether the entry point into gospel culture for many pastors and churches will be through coming to enjoy this matter of honesty. When we're honest with each other, I feel trusted. I feel honored. I would not violate that trust for all the world.

See the Glory!

A Culture of Gospel Honor

Outdo one another in showing honor.

ROMANS 12:10

EVERY TUESDAY EVENING for many years, Immanuel Church in Nashville hosted an event we called Immanuel Theology for Men. During the first hour, I (Ray) taught the men the Bible and theology. We plowed through the book of Romans, for example. It was teaching more than preaching—interactive, thoughtful, and fun. That was our first hour together. Then in our second hour, we transitioned to a time of gospel honesty and "walking in the light," as I unpacked for you in chapter 3. Men would gather in pairs. They didn't hang back in the shadows of denial and conceal-ment but came right out and walked together in openness. One guy would turn to the other and say something like, "So, here's how I'm not doing well," or, "Here's the sin I need to confess." Then he'd talk about it with his friend. His friend wouldn't "fix" him or even necessarily advise him. Instead, he'd quietly listen and then say, "Thanks. Let's pray." After he prayed, the two men would turn it around. The second guy would walk in the light and be prayed for.

We'd all come together again, in the last half hour or so, for "honor time." That was when the men would openly and sincerely "outdo one another in showing honor" (Rom. 12:10). It's what the gospel does. Specifically, *the doctrine of glorification* creates a culture of honor.

In Paul's letter to the Romans, we see a surprise coming down from above: God isn't out merely to make us nicer. His heart is set on making us *glorious forever*. God's grace redefines our future with bold expressions like "glory and honor and immortality" (2:7), "the glory of the children of God" (8:21), "the redemption of our bodies" (8:23), and "those whom he justified he also glorified" (8:30).

If the touchdown God plans to score for us is nothing less than our *glorification*—with Christ, like Christ, in a sparkling new universe forever—then it's no surprise that our glorious future brightens up our dreary present. It's no surprise, moreover, that Paul urges us, "Outdo one another in showing honor" (12:10). This is far more than niceness; it's dignity, respect, gratitude, and esteem—for starters! And how could it be otherwise, as we learn to see one another with gospel-illuminated eyes?

Strikingly, the command of Romans 12:10 is not merely to honor one another but to *outdo* one another in showing honor. It's competitive, and everyone wins! The hope of the gospel frees our hearts from brooding self-focus, leaving us with nothing to give to others. Instead, we look around at one another, and we start coming alive to "Christ in *you*, the hope of glory" (Col. 1:27).

See the Glory in One Another

Here's how it looked during "honor time." Back together again as a group, I'd briefly explain Romans 12:10 as I did above, and then I'd open it up to the guys. Immediately, men raised their hands and jumped right into affirming, thanking, and recognizing one another in true and significant ways.

For example, one guy might say to another, right in front of everyone:

Jim, I honor you because last Friday night when I texted you and told you I really wanted to go back to porn, you called me immediately and talked me off that cliff. You didn't have to call. But you did. And it took twenty minutes. But I couldn't have made it through without you. Dude, I honor you!

The vibe in the room was powerful. It was the gospel the men were experiencing. And by nine o'clock every Tuesday evening, men were taught, men were safe, and men were honored. It didn't take long until sarcastic put-downs became *unthinkable*. Gospel doctrine created gospel culture where men, with no gimmicks and no hype, dared to believe the reality of their salvation so deeply that they built a community of honor together. It flavored our whole church. The good news of our glorification came down vertically to us and spread out horizontally among us, and we start treating one another like royalty.

Who wouldn't flourish in an environment like that? In today's predatory world, people cut each other down to size every day. Some of us have never known anything else, even in our homes growing up. But how different is a healthy church! There we lift each other up, not with empty flattery but with real honor because real glory is beginning to appear. Let's notice it! Let's celebrate it! The eschaton is becoming visible right now in the saints around us. How could we keep quiet about *that*?

So why not give ourselves permission to see the other Christians right around us with gospel eyes? Let's marvel at them—what they are and what they will be. We don't have to pretend. All we have to do is believe the gospel and let its hope-inspiring promise set the tone of our relationships. Let's defy whatever petty and unworthy barriers hold us back. Let's allow the doctrine of glorification to create a culture of honor wherever we live, for as long as we live. *It might start feeling like revival.*

See with King David's Eyes

This beautiful way of seeing one another goes all the way back to the Old Testament. Check this out:

> As for the saints in the land, they are the excellent ones,
>   in whom is all my delight. (Ps. 16:3)

We're walking through the double privilege of grace. Not only do we get to spend our lives delighting in the Lord Jesus because he delights in us. Not only do we come to him, holding out empty hands of faith, and he rejoices to give us his best: justification, sanctification, and glorification—all of grace. But as we come to him, we also notice in our peripheral vision that many others are coming too. To our astonishment, we discover that we are now included not only in the heart of Christ but also in "the communion of saints." Whatever they look like on the outside, they are excellent on the inside because Christ lives in them.

Psalm 16:3 is the voice of one believer, King David of old, building a culture of honor with other believers in his generation. He is essentially telling us, "Here is the difference the gospel makes in *me* as I notice *them*."

"As for the saints in the land . . ." Who are "the saints"? They aren't the standout players on God's team while the rest of us underachievers sit on the bench. *All* of us are saints because we are all set apart to God in Christ (1 Cor. 1:2). *You* are a saint. God chose you before you chose him. His love for you created your love for him. Your future is defined by his purpose and not by your performance. The most noteworthy thing about you is not you but God's love for you. We sometimes try to set ourselves apart by our accomplishments, but what could be greater about you than what God has accomplished *for* you and promised *to* you? His grace is your dignity, and his grace will not fail you.

You, saintly sinner—sinner now, saintly forever—are "in the land" even now because you are "in Christ." Around 160 times in the New Testament, we encounter this striking way of speaking about the difference Jesus makes for us. Paul's insight is so audacious that he had to invent the expression *in Christ* to get it across. We call it "union with Christ." We aren't just *near* him, but we are *in* him, like branches in a vine (John 15:1–5). This doesn't mean we are *blurred into* Christ, but it does mean we're *inseparable from* all the benefits and advantages we receive in Christ. *God has so removed every barrier by his grace* that you are included, you belong, and you have a new address in God's promised land, a *permanent* new address where your future will unfold forever.

His promised land is a big place. Lots of people live there. Lots of tribes and groups and looks, but all one in Christ (Gal. 3:28). He gives us more in common than we have in distinction. We're not a club where only "our type of people" belong. We are his community where he defines who's in, who's "kosher," and he *loves* to make natural enemies into new friends. When you meet a Christian you wouldn't naturally like, you can praise God because you are encountering in human form the love of God that is greater than your love—great enough to include you too!

Okay then. Here is where the gospel takes us. We start perceiving one another with a sense of *awe*. The phrase "as for the saints in the land" opens our eyes to the people around us at church every single Sunday, not simply as members of that church but also as members of Christ himself. God has deeply included them too. And his new community, embodied at your church, is heaven's gift to a hellish world. Your church is a holy, sacred, blood-bought *glory* in the making. Your church is how Jesus gives his felt presence to your city. Let's all hold ourselves to the highest standards of integrity in all our churches, for we—yes, even we—are together his saints.

"*. . . they are the excellent ones . . .*" Every single believer in Jesus is *fascinating*. It typically takes only twenty or thirty seconds in a conversation to start seeing the glory. Just ask leading questions like, "So, tell me your story. Where did you grow up? How did you get here?" And as you stand there listening, the excellencies begin to appear. You're thinking, "Wow, this person's story has

God's fingerprints all over it!" The same goes for you too. You have a story to tell of his grace redirecting you toward a glorious destiny. You are not shabby, second rate, or small. You too are an excellent one. Go ahead and believe it. You aren't the exception. You haven't defeated God's grace. And if his excellent grace has reached even you, then every other Christian you know stands within the same circle of grace you stand in. Every Christian you know is destined for the eternal glory you too stand to inherit.

This strong adjective, *excellent*, in Psalm 16:3 can also be translated "magnificent, prominent, glorious." David is basically saying, "I *admire* God's people. They are the true royalty in this world. Whoever they are, whatever their race or class or position, however ordinary they may appear for now, God has lifted them up. With all their flaws, at a deeper level, they belong to him. And his grace, setting them apart to himself, makes their ambitions loftier, their convictions deeper, their sufferings nobler, their laughter brighter, their delights purer. God has destined them for eternal greatness, and it's appearing in them even in this life. Truly, the world is not worthy of them." C. S. Lewis pointed out that if we could see now how even the humblest saint will be glorified in heaven, then we'd be tempted to fall down in worship.[1] Truly, "they are the excellent ones."

"*. . . in whom is all my delight.*" Now David takes the next step, and it's a bold, personal, emotional step. "As for the saints in the land" is David acknowledging the reality of God's grace at work among his people. "They are the excellent ones" is David being attentive and fair-minded, so that he notices the glimmers

---

1   C. S. Lewis, *The Weight of Glory and Other Addresses* (1941; repr., Grand Rapids, MI: Eerdmans, 1974), 15.

of coming glory in God's people, "the hope of glory" that Paul alerts us to in Colossians 1:27. But now, in his final phrase, David allows no hint of aloof detachment and openly declares his personal commitment. With "in whom is all my delight," he is saying, "I'm all in! If they're God's people, they're my people, and I give them my whole heart."

Charles Spurgeon felt this way. Not long after his conversion, his heart was so changed by God's grace that he could say,

> I felt that I could not be happy without fellowship with the people of God. I wanted to be wherever they were, and if anybody ridiculed them, I wished to be ridiculed with them, and if people had an ugly name for them, I wanted to be called by that ugly name, for I felt that, unless I suffered with Christ in his humiliation, I could not expect to reign with him in his glory.[2]

The truth of the gospel is so intertwined with the communion of saints that Schaeffer used to speak of "the two orthodoxies," the orthodoxy of doctrine and *orthodoxy of community*.[3] Spurgeon, therefore, was truly orthodox, wasn't he? Both his head and his heart, both his teaching and his relationships were aligned with the biblical gospel of glorification. If we today stand proudly for our strong doctrine while we settle for weak relationships, then can we please have the decency to shut up about orthodoxy? But far better, could we have the humility to embrace the gospel in

---

2   C. H. Spurgeon, *Autobiography*, vol., 1, *The Early Years, 1834–1859* (1897; repr., Edinburgh: Banner of Truth, 1985), 145.

3   Francis A. Schaeffer, *Two Contents, Two Realities* (Downers Grove, IL: InterVarsity Press, 1975), 26.

both doctrine and culture and, by God's grace, start walking in newness of life like Spurgeon, David, and all the true saints of all the ages?

"In whom is all my delight" is a decisive commitment. David's language might even sound borderline idolatrous. If David had said, as he often does, "The Lord is all my delight," then we would think, "Of course." But Psalm 16:3 takes us to a new place together, a place of openly stated, joyously emphatic, wholehearted, and unashamed enthusiasm for one another. Psalm 16:3 doesn't allow us to hold back and play it safe. Psalm 16:3 calls us to come together for Jesus's sake, noticing the best in one another and expressing our admiration for what we see. "As for the saints in the land, they are the excellent ones, / *in whom is all my delight.*"

Give Your Heart Away

The Bible says the early church met together "with glad and generous hearts" (Acts 2:46). They *enjoyed* being together. They gave themselves to one another fully and openly, the way David gave his heart away. Some people never do that. They're careful not to go too far in vulnerability and devotion to others. They never give their hearts away. Instead, they live in self-protection, and they role-play relationships. But the gospel calls and commands us to fling away all such tragic limitations and gladly lose something of ourselves for the sake of the saints around us.

Have you given yourself away to the people around you? Have you recognized that you and they are diminished without one another? Or do you stand back and size up others with critical detachment and a wait-and-see attitude? The word "my" in "in whom is all *my* delight" makes a *personal* claim on every one of us, doesn't it?

Christ has given his heart to us. Let's give our hearts to one another. And if you're thinking, "But my church is a mess," well, what church isn't a mess? But it's *his* mess, and his glory is there too. Heaven keeps sneaking into our churches, showing up in flawed people like every one of us. The Lord himself is there in your church. He put you there too. You and your church believe the gospel. So, you're already equipped in every essential for the display of his glory together.

You don't need to find more money in your budget. You don't need to pass a motion in a meeting. You don't need to change to a different denomination. Just believe the gospel, help your people to believe the gospel, and take one step after another into a joyous culture of honor. Sure, some people won't respond as readily as you'd like, but don't let that stop you. Others will respond gladly, and the joy will catch on.

Paul wrote to his Christian friends: "What is our hope or joy or crown of boasting before our Lord Jesus at his coming? Is it not you? For you are our glory and joy" (1 Thess. 2:19–20). Amazing, isn't it? Paul was essentially saying, "What do I want out of this life? What's my reward? *Is it not you?*" We're so bound together in Christ that both our life stories now and our final reward in the future are enriched by our solidarity together as friends in Christ.

What Will It Take?

Pastor, maybe you need to rejoin your church. In your heart, maybe you need to re-up with your people. Maybe the disappointments of ministry have allowed you to pull your heart back. Maybe it's time to hurl yourself again into the ups and downs of your church family. Their shortcomings cannot erase the doctrine of glorification, so they cannot prevent a culture of honorable and honoring solidarity.

In 1836, First Presbyterian Church of Augusta, Georgia, where I (Ray) served as senior pastor years ago, was deciding whether to buy an organ. Some members wanted it. Others opposed it. In the congregational meeting to settle the question, one man, Mr. Campbell, rose to demand chapter and verse in the Bible that "gave authority for the worship of God with machinery!" Okay. Good point. But the majority voted in favor, and so a certain Mr. Gould was chosen to raise the money for the new organ. One day these two men happened to meet in downtown Augusta. Mr. Campbell asked Mr. Gould why he hadn't contacted him for a donation. "Because I knew you did not wish to have the organ," was the answer.

"That makes no difference," Mr. Campbell said. "When the majority of the members have decided the matter, it is my duty to put aside personal feeling and assist as well as I may."[4]

Way to go, Mr. Campbell! Losing a vote only means greater opportunity for selfless nobility, glory, and honor, through Jesus and for his sake.

Pastor, you are a carrier of that healthy contagion—that life-giving gospel that is spreading all over the world today. You're not wearing a mask, and the gospel conviction and comfort coming out of your mouth are helping everyone around you get healthy together. Keep on, and keep on, and keep on!

4 David B. Calhoun, *Cloud of Witnesses: The Story of First Presbyterian Church, Augusta, Georgia, 1804–2004* (Augusta, GA: First Presbyterian Church, 2004), 41–42.

Discussion Questions

1. As you read chapter 4, what was the one insight that stood out to you most, and why?

2. What is it deep inside us all that shrinks from openly honoring one another for the real evidence of divine grace that is visible and even obvious? What misunderstandings of Jesus and his gospel might hold us back?

3. What practical steps can your church take to set a new tone of sincerely honoring one another for real faithfulness to the Lord?

Calling Russell Moore

Ray: I have never in all my life met anyone who was too encouraged in Christ. We're not in any danger of being too encouraged in Christ. Churches typically live on a starvation diet of encouragement and honor. But we can stop the starving because there's a feast awaiting us.

Sam: Every culture has its own way of undermining honor, whether it's the sort of English reserve, the "I'll literally die before I tell you that I love you" kind of thing, or the Southern US flattery. But we need to step into a culture of honor intentionally because we're not going to drift into it, are we?

Ray: I totally agree with that, Sam. Who wouldn't love to be a part of a manly, bold culture of honor where serious men get together with both their flaws and their glories and we share it all together. Pastor, you can do this. If you long for this, you're not crazy. You're being drawn along by the Holy Spirit of God, and Sam and I are just glad to encourage you and help you along the way.

Sam: Why don't we just do this now? Why don't we call one of our mutual friends, someone we both adore and revere and honor him? I'll see if he's around.

Russell Moore: Hello?

Sam: Hi, Russell. This is Sam Allberry. I'm here with Ray Ortlund. Ray and I are recording a conversation for our podcast, *You're Not Crazy*. We've just been talking about Paul's instructions to honor one another, and you came to mind because you're a mutual friend of both Ray's and mine. We wanted to quickly get a hold of you and tell you how much you mean to us.

Ray: Russell, this is always awkward between us men, but you're going to have to deal with it. Now, listen. Here's why I honor Russell Moore. Two things come to mind immediately. He's a consistent witness marked by integrity and courage, both of which are all too rare among Christian leaders. I've been watching you walk with integrity and courage for years. There is evidence of supernatural grace within and upon you. You have inspired me countless times without realizing it because when I'm facing difficulty, trouble, and distress, the thought comes to me, "Wait a minute, I don't have to give up. I don't have to give in. Russell Moore is out there, and he's still going. He's marked by integrity and courage. I can do this by God's grace and for his glory too.

Sam: Thanks, Ray. Russell, I just wanted to say that I look at what you've had to endure in your ministry, and you've not run away from the Lord's work. You've not become a bitter, cynical guy. I was looking at Paul honoring Epaphroditus in Philippians 2 and what Epaphroditus suffered for his service of Christ. It made me realize how much you've endured and how much we owe you for that. So, thank you for serving us, even when it's been very costly.

Russell: That means more than I can communicate because I would not have been able to be in ministry over the last several years if not for the two of you. The Lord arranged just the right conversation, just the right call, just the right encouragement at just the right time, and I needed it. So that makes me all the more grateful.

Ray: Well, we love you. Thank you for letting us interrupt your day.

Let Christ Preach

A Culture of Gospel Invitation

*He came and preached peace to you who were
far off and peace to those who were near.*

EPHESIANS 2:17

LOOKING AT PICTURES from your younger days can be humbling. I (Sam) have a picture of myself, around ten years old, with spiky hair and mismatched fluorescent socks. I'm not sure I can blame my bad taste on late-1980s fashion. I think it was just me. Pictures from subsequent years seem to confirm that analysis.

I have the same feeling looking at some of my old sermons.

I was recently invited to preach on a text in Acts. As I prepared, I had a sense of déjà vu. I checked my files and realized I'd preached the passage before. This came as a relief. I was short on preparation time, and modifying an old sermon is easier than writing a new one. But the relief was short-lived. When I looked through my old manuscript, I saw that it wasn't a train wreck. I wasn't preaching anything contrary to the text, and there were some genuinely helpful insights. But something wasn't right. I dug out some other sermons from the same period to see how they compared. With each, I came to the same unhappy conclusion: too much exegesis and not enough Jesus.

Ouch.

My view of what makes a good sermon—like my view of what constitutes good clothing—has changed over the years. In those early days, I thought of preaching primarily as "teaching the Bible." My job was to tell people what the passage said, to transfer scriptural data from my head into other people's brains. This isn't wholly wrong. But it's also far from wholly right.

Preach the Text, Don't *Just* Preach the Text

Yes, the Bible is our authority. We have nowhere else to turn. We dare not preach anything else, and it's crucially important to get the text right. After all, it matters how precious things are handled.

Many years ago, I had an abscess that formed on the scar of an appendectomy. It bulged out and was spectacularly painful, even if lightly touched. A fly landing on it would pretty much have me yelping. So, when the attending doctor asked if I'd mind if he brought some medical students in to take a look—apparently it was a great test case for their diagnostic skills—I was somewhat wary. With good reason. The first student began to clumsily prod my chest, slowly working his way toward my abdomen to see where I might be experiencing pain. I didn't let him get far, protesting that even a fraction of the pressure he'd used so far, if applied to the abscess, would send me into exquisite pain (and possibly him to the emergency room). The doctor swiftly halted the examination, telling the student this would have failed him had it been a clinical exam.

A problematic abdomen is not the only thing that needs to be handled carefully. Scripture does too—not because it is problematic but because we are. As Paul encourages Timothy, "Do your best to present yourself to God as one approved, a worker who has no need to be ashamed, rightly handling the word of truth" (2 Tim. 2:15). It's not enough to handle God's word; we must handle it *rightly*. It's alarmingly possible to use a passage in a way that's unfaithful to its intent. As David Helm says, "Some preachers use the Bible the way a drunk uses a lamp post . . . more for support than for illumination."[1] In other words, there's a difference between being *Bible-based* and being *biblical*. Being Bible-based is simply using Scripture, often just a verse or two, to justify what you're saying, but being biblical is making sure what you're saying is true to what Scripture *as a whole* says.

Entire churches and denominations have drifted from Christ because the Bible wasn't rightly handled. This happened in the UK in the mid- to late twentieth century. Dick Lucas, who was Rector of St. Helen's, Bishopsgate in the City of London, from 1961–1998, was able to see what was going wrong in much of the preaching around him: even well-meaning preachers were missing the point of Bible passages. So, he set about organizing

---

1   David Helm, *Expositional Preaching: How We Speak God's Word Today* (Wheaton, IL: Crossway, 2014), 24.

preaching conferences to address the deficits. This eventually led to the launch of the Cornhill Training Course, which focused on helping preachers learn the practical skills needed to understand and communicate what the Bible says.

I was privileged to attend the Cornhill Training Course in the late 1990s, and I'll go to my grave deeply thankful for the exegetical skills I learned there. Yet after the course, I somehow ended up thinking that getting the passage right was the main task of the preacher. Once I'd done the exegetical work, I thought I'd done the bulk of my sermon preparation. But getting the Scripture right, while essential, is not sufficient. It's not enough to simply explain the text. More is needed. Failing to see that led to many years of preaching that now leave me wincing.

James gives us this stark warning: "You believe that God is one; you do well. Even the demons believe—and shudder!" (James 2:19). The belief that God is one is not a trivial part of Christian doctrine; it is foundational. Old Testament believers recited the truth that God is one in the Shema every day. The same truth is given pride of place in the great creeds of the Christian church: "We believe in one God." But even *demons* believe this. Apparently, there's a form of orthodox theology in hell. So, before we congratulate ourselves on having sound doctrine, we need to remember that believing the right, scriptural things isn't enough.

Jesus gave a similar warning in a text that should haunt any church that seeks to be scriptural: "You search the Scriptures because you think that in them you have eternal life; and it is they that bear witness about me, yet you refuse to come to me that you may have life" (John 5:39). We might instinctively applaud the Pharisees for how Jesus describes them here. They diligently study the Scriptures; we long for that to be true of everyone in our churches. They know that eternal life is found in the Scriptures; that's also great. Scripture is not about merely theoretical or academic concerns; life and eternity are at stake. Yet it's possible to get this far without coming to Jesus. We should tremble at such a frightening thought. We can have Bible-studying and eternal-life-pursuing churches that miss out on Jesus entirely.

We must be careful that our attentiveness to the text doesn't become an end in itself. Preaching is not just a matter of helping people add to their Bible knowledge. Nor is it simply about trying to give people a particular experience.

Don't Preach Yourself

I remember a preacher I heard from time to time who was spellbinding. He was funny and poignant. He'd *wow* us every time. We'd pour out of church talking about how great the sermon was. But come Monday morning, I'd never remember what the sermon was *about*. I'd been moved by it, but I'd struggle to put my finger on what I'd been moved *by*. There had been powerful anecdotes aplenty, but I'm not sure he was *teaching* us anything.

I'm not naturally a captivating speaker. When I'm preaching at another church, the tech guys sometimes ask how much of the stage I'm likely to utilize while I preach so that they can figure out camera angles. I tell them they won't need to pan at all. The most I'll likely move is to shift weight from one foot to the other. I'm just not that expressive. You may know those famous silhouettes of Charles Simeon preaching back in the nineteenth century, with his head and arms struck in various expressive postures. If someone produced one of those of me preaching, it'd be the same image in each frame.

But there is comfort in the fact that the apostle Paul may not have been the most skilled public speaker:

> For they say, "His letters are weighty and strong, but his bodily presence is weak, and his speech of no account." (2 Cor. 10:10)

> Even if I am unskilled in speaking, I am not so in knowledge; indeed, in every way we have made this plain to you in all things. (2 Cor. 11:6)

Even by his own admission, Paul wasn't the most compelling speaker by worldly standards. So there's no reason to despair if we feel lacking. To use us, God doesn't need us to have the most eloquent voices in town.

Even though there's a part of me that has wanted to be a more dynamic communicator, I'm glad I don't have the gift of gab. For as lovely as it would be to routinely hold a crowd in rapt attention, it's healthy to not be able to do so. If I knew I could captivate people by my own natural charisma, it would be too tempting, and I might not work as hard at understanding and preaching the text as I should. Instead, I must work hard on what I'm saying. The content of my sermon must be compelling, or I feel I have no reason to be there. If the word isn't moving anyone, I've no reason to think I will.

So, if preaching isn't simply transferring data or trying to make people feel something through our charisma, what is it?

A New Covenant Vision of Preaching[2]

The New Testament zeros in on a fourfold vision of preaching. Let's unpack it.

First, we're preaching Jesus. Paul writes, "Him we proclaim, warning everyone and teaching everyone with all wisdom, that we may present everyone mature in Christ" (Col. 1:28). We're not just teaching the Bible or explaining a passage. We're not just giving people information about Jesus. We're *proclaiming* him. The content of our preaching is a person. The church is not just hearing a message; they are meeting the Savior. Whatever else our sermon is about, it's ultimately meant to be about him.

Second, we're proclaiming the unfathomably good Jesus. Hear the apostle again: "To me, though I am the very least of all the saints, this grace was given, to preach to the Gentiles the unsearchable riches of Christ" (Eph. 3:8). As we seek to proclaim Jesus, we need to ensure it's *this* unsearchably rich Jesus we're proclaiming.

There are a lot of Jesuses out there. There's the here-to-fulfill-your-dreams Jesus. There's the constantly-scolding-you-to-do-better Jesus. There's the I-only-care-about-social-issues Jesus. But the only Jesus that matters is the Jesus who is *there*. Paul says he's the Jesus of "unsearchable riches." In other words, the Jesus we're to proclaim is *unfathomably* good. We'll never get our heads around it. We're to preach him in a way that makes it so apparent that there is no one else in the universe like this man. When we preach this way, our affections are now in play.

2   Portions in this section are adapted from Sam Allberry, "Ephesians 2 Wrecked My View of Preaching," The Gospel Coalition (website), October 2, 2021, https://www.thegospelcoalition.org/.

Third, we're bringing people to the crucified Christ. "O foolish Galatians!" Paul scolded. "Who has bewitched you? It was before your eyes that Jesus Christ was publicly portrayed as crucified" (Gal. 3:1). Jesus's immeasurable riches come to us through his death. So, we cannot proclaim him without proclaiming him as crucified.

But notice how even this is not simply telling people *about* his death. As Paul preached the cross, the people were able to *see* it. It wasn't merely a historical data point put before their minds; it was an existential reality before their eyes. But don't misunderstand. Paul wasn't drawing pictures on a flip chart; he was proclaiming the cross with such immediacy that it was as if the Galatians were *there* at the foot of the cross. They had been transported.

Finally, Christ himself is proclaiming Christ. These verses I've referenced above have blown apart my understanding of preaching over the years. But there's one that has wrecked preaching for me. A few years ago, I was reading through Ephesians, minding my own business, when I read this: "And he came and preached peace to you who were far off and peace to those who were near" (Eph. 2:17). Paul writes here about how the message of the gospel first came to his readers in Ephesus. "You who were far off" is Paul's way of talking about Gentiles; "those who were near," the Jews. The Christian community in Ephesus was made up of both groups, and wonderfully, the same gospel of peace had come to each. Moreover, "far off" and "near" function together as a *merism*, a figure of speech that combines opposites to express totality. Until Christ comes again, the sermon that is preached to everyone everywhere is peace. Indeed, Paul's wider point is that the gospel has made all people (but especially these two distinct groups) into one new humanity. Jesus created not just a new community but a new *kind* of community to which Jew and Gentile alike fully and equally belong.

But what struck me as I read Ephesians 2:17 was not so much the gospel of peace but who was preaching it: "*He* came and preached peace to you." *Christ* came and preached to the Ephesians.

This raises a question: *When?*

Ephesus is in modern-day Turkey, around one thousand miles from Jesus's regular haunts in Galilee. Was there an unrecorded moment in Jesus's earthly ministry when he popped across the Mediterranean for a quick preaching tour in Asia minor? No. Christ came and preached when the *gospel itself* first came to Ephesus. When Paul and his colleagues proclaimed the Christian message, *Christ himself* came and preached peace to the Ephesians.

This is staggering. Paul and others were the speakers, but Jesus was the preacher. Consider that. Paul has already said that Christ "himself is our peace" (2:14). In him is all the harmonizing fullness of God's shalom. He is the integrating center of all things. In him all the parts finally fit together, and life comes into a deep and liberating cohesion. We will never find ultimate peace outside him. Jesus is our peace. This means he was both the one preaching and the one being preached—both the means and the message, the communicator and the content, the speaker and the sermon.

All those years ago in dusty, ancient Ephesus, as Paul and others labored away, making the case for Jesus, answering objections, fielding hostile questions, and explaining gospel truth to the uninterested, the confused, and the searching alike—in all this *Christ was preaching Christ* to the men and women in Ephesus.

Through his fallible, human servants, Jesus preaches Jesus to the hearts of those who listen.

How could we ever want anything less than this for our preaching? When we open the word of God to the people of God, our longing is for Christ himself to come and make himself known to the hearts of those listening. That he would be preaching. That he would be who people remember.

Christ's Presence Changes Preaching

The presence of Christ in preaching has changed so many aspects of the task for me.

Christ's presence has changed what I'm praying for. Pastors, let's give up our small ambitions. I no longer want people to just understand the passage, or even to merely hear God's word. My longing is that Christ would present himself in all his unsearchable goodness to all listening—that we'd be conscious of his presence in the room, that we'd know his voice and his life-changing love.

Christ's presence has changed how I prepare. I work no less with the text, seeking to handle it rightly. I exegete as carefully and faithfully as I can. But that is now just one part of the task and not my sole focus. As I seek to understand the text in its context, the main questions before me are not, What does this mean? or, How can this change us? Now I'm asking, How is this text, in all its particularity, wanting to wow me with Jesus? What fresh reason does it give me to worship and adore him?

We all have a favorite place on the planet, somewhere that stirs our soul with its natural beauty. Yours might be Caribbean beaches or Alpine majesty. Mine is the Isle of Skye, one of the inner Hebridean islands off the coast of northwest Scotland. Even the word *Hebridean* conjures images of purple hills wreathed in cloud, moss-covered rocks, and wine-dark pools. The first time a friend of mine and I visited Skye, our conversation in the car seemed to consist entirely of saying "wow" in unison. Each time we crested a hill or rounded a bend, some new incomprehensible beauty would heave into view. No matter how far we drove, the scenery kept wowing us.

I've found the same to be true of Jesus as I've read Scripture. Each text, section, genre, and book—every part of the scriptural landscape is wowing us with Jesus. There's always more to see and discover. It's always wonderful. There are no diminishing returns with him. No hidden disappointments. Just unending and ever-increasing beauty and goodness. This is what our preaching should convey. He's *always* better than we thought he was.

Which has changed my view of sermon feedback too. I once loved it if someone said to me at the church door, "You're an amazing preacher." Don't get me wrong: that's still better than "You're a terrible preacher." But it doesn't come close to the feedback that matters most. Better is "What an amazing passage." At least the focus is now on God's word rather than on the preacher. I like it when someone talks about a past sermon and remembers the text more than they remember who preached it. But the best feedback is "What an amazing Savior!" That's what we're working for. That's what it's all about. Then Jesus is the one they're wowed by. He's the one they come away remembering.

Finally, the vision of Christ preaching Christ significantly changes sermon application. It means our preaching doesn't always have to be "challenging." We want preaching to change people. We know God's word has the power to do just that. But our instincts tell us people need to be *pushed* ahead in their discipleship, that each week we need to give them something to work on, something to do, something to take home and make progress with. We're looking for results, and our preaching is meant to be the agency for this.

Yes, preaching is meant to change us. But perhaps not the way we instinctively think. Paul's letter to Titus helps us here:

> For the grace of God has appeared that offers salvation to all people. It teaches us to say "No" to ungodliness and worldly passions, and to live self-controlled, upright and godly lives in this present age. (Titus 2:11–12 NIV)

God has always been gracious. Throughout the Old Testament, his pinned tweet was "The LORD, the LORD, a God merciful and gracious, slow to anger, and abounding in steadfast love and faithfulness" (Ex. 34:6). This is who he has always been. But now, Paul tells us, the coming of Jesus is the appearing of grace. Grace himself has appeared in human form and offered salvation.

That grace is what teaches us to say no to ungodliness and sin. His kindness leads us to repentance (Rom. 2:4).

Grace is not like a runway, the thing that launches us off. Grace is the plane itself. We get nowhere apart from God's grace. If a believer isn't turning from sin, he doesn't need more tasering from the preacher; he needs more exposure to the grace of God. It's grace that changes us.

I sometimes think of it this way: I like orange juice first thing in the morning, but I don't like it just after I've brushed my teeth. Why? The juice hasn't changed. My palate has. The presence of toothpaste changes the taste buds, and now orange juice seems horribly sour. Something similar happens as we taste God's grace in Christ. It affects our moral taste buds. Sin begins to lose its flavor.

How We *Really* Change

Preaching that will produce deep and lasting heart-level change is preaching that continually opens our core to God's grace. If this is true, we must move from a model of grace-*then*-pressure (the pressure being the key agent of change) to a preaching model that shows people how grace itself reorients our hearts, so we *want* to devote ourselves to Christ.

Several Sundays ago, I preached on John 12:1–11. I wanted to drill down into what Mary did for Jesus:

> Mary therefore took a pound of expensive ointment made from pure nard, and anointed the feet of Jesus and wiped his feet with her hair. The house was filled with the fragrance of the perfume. (John 12:3)

John wants us to see how Mary lavishly honors Jesus. He goes into unusual detail: expensive ointment made from pure nard, which is a rare item imported from north India. It was high-end stuff. As Judas points out, it was worth about a day's wages. Ointment this expensive might be treated as an heirloom and passed down through the family. It was a form of capital. If it was ever used at all, it would be for a special occasion, and even then only sparingly. Yet Mary seems to tip the whole lot over Jesus.

It's not just the amount but the manner of the anointing that's unusual. Normally you'd just anoint the head; she anoints Jesus's feet, a particularly dirty part of the body back then. She then uses her hair to wipe his feet. Hair was the opposite end of the body to the feet, not just physically but in terms of cleanliness. Not only that, but hair was generally kept tied up in social contexts like this. Yet Mary lets hers down and uses it as a rag. With her ointment, she's using what's most costly to her and applying it to what's most lowly of him. With her hair, she's using the cleanest part of her for the dirtiest part of him. All this breaks multiple social conventions, causes embarrassment and awkwardness to those around, and provokes strong words of rebuke. Yet Jesus commends her, telling Judas to "leave her alone" (12:7).

In the initial draft of my sermon, I went for the challenge: Do we adore Jesus like she does? Are we prepared to give up what is most costly to us? To create social awkwardness? Are we willing to not fit in on account of our devotion to him? How much do you *actually* love him? Such questions drive the congregation's attention inward and press each person toward a negative answer. It's a Christian exam you just failed. Go away and think about it and do better next time. Such challenges leave us deflated, defeated, and feeling like we're never going to change.

But then I thought, "Don't challenge. Invite." Rather than using the passage to expose how insufficiently we love Jesus, why not use it to give people reason to love him more?

So, I rewrote the application, framing it differently: Look at how precious Jesus is to Mary. There's something to see in Jesus that can so capture our hearts that he's worth our highest adoration, worth any social embarrassment that comes from people knowing we love him, worth not fitting in. He's worth all these things because he's *better* than all these things. And it's his death for us that most brings it into view. He would give up something far costlier than even pure nard, prompt more awkwardness than merely breaking social convention, and face not fitting in to the extent of enduring physical torture and a shameful death—for us. Death stinks, in every sense (John has just reminded us of that, 11:39). But now this house is filled with the fragrance of a different kind of death (12:3)—a death that becomes beautiful to us, not because it was in any way sanitized (quite the opposite) but because of the love it expressed and the life it won for us.

That's a different kind of application. Now our attention is on Jesus rather than ourselves, on his glorious grace rather than our dismal performance. Now we *want* to give him our all.

Preach Imperatives with Gospel Light

I think I blew it the following Sunday. My text this time was from Romans:

> Do not present your members to sin as instruments for un-righteousness, but present yourselves to God as those who have been brought from death to life, and your members to God as instruments for righteousness. (Rom. 6:13)

Later in the letter, Paul will tell us that offering our "bodies as a living sacrifice" (Rom. 12:1) is how we should respond to God's mercy. Here in Romans 6, we get an anticipation of what that involves. Offering our bodies includes offering their various parts. So, I taught this passage as a set of "oughts": we *ought* to offer our various physical capacities to him—our eyes so we might see the world as God does, our feet so we might go where there is need, our tongues so our words might lift up rather than tear down.

In one sense, that's true. The New Testament is full of commands that we are to obey. Many passages confront us. Back in chapter 1, we saw how Paul rebuked Peter. There will also be times when we need to do what Scripture says even if we don't feel like it. Jesus's words have especially helped me see this:

> As the Father has loved me, so have I loved you. Abide in my love. If you keep my commandments, you will abide in my love, just as I have kept my Father's commandments and abide in his love. These things I have spoken to you, that my joy may be in you, and that your joy may be full. (John 15:9–11)

At first glance, it might seem Jesus is saying obedience is what makes him love us.[3] Not at all. He gives his love to us freely and lavishly through his death and resurrection. And once we receive that love, we mustn't rush off and leave it. We're to stay put and remain in it, to bask in it. And to bask in Jesus's love, obedience is key. As we obey what he's commanded, we have ongoing exposure to his love for us. Every single thing our King calls us to do expresses his goodness and care. As we walk with the Lord more and more, we see the goodness of his ways. To follow, even initially through gritted teeth, is a declaration of trust in God, who knows more than we do. Rather than thinking we'll obey when we like it, we should instead resolve to obey *so that* we like it.

---

3   This paragraph is adapted from Sam Allberry, "Do You Have to Like God's Commands?" The Gospel Coalition (website), November 14, 2016, https://www.thegospel coalition.org/.

So, we're not to deny the imperatival force of the commands in Scripture. But we are to see how those commands flow directly from the gospel itself.

Let's look again at Romans 6. Paul tells us we're not to offer our body parts to sin as instruments of unrighteousness, not just because it's an easy possibility in fallen bodies but because it's precisely what marked our preconversion life. Earlier in Romans, when Paul showed us that "all [alike] are under sin," he used examples of how our various parts had been pressed into sin's service:

Their throat is an open grave;
    they use their tongues to deceive.
The venom of asps is under their lips.
    Their mouth is full of curses and bitterness.
Their feet are swift to shed blood;
    in their paths are ruin and misery,
and the way of peace they have not known.
    There is no fear of God before their eyes. (Rom. 3:13–18)

These parts that we used for sin over and over can now be offered to God. He'll accept them. He'll even *use* them.

A friend who was preparing to marry confessed his past sexual sin was so great that he wondered whether he'd ever be able to glorify God with this part of life. He'd so misused his sexuality in the past. But the grace of Jesus is so expansive in its redemptive work that even body parts that have been used only for wickedness can now be used for God's glory. In this way, Romans 6 shows us not only that we're *meant* to offer our body parts to God but that we *get* to. They're not a write-off. They can be "instruments for righteousness."

Gospel Vision Is the Key to Obedience

The key to application is the gospel itself. The gospel is not far away over there with obedience as an entirely separate part of the Christian life. No, application is letting the grace of Christ work itself out in our lives at the granular level.

I love how John puts it:

> Beloved, we are God's children now, and what we will be has not yet appeared; but we know that when he appears we shall be like him, because we shall see him as he is. And everyone who thus hopes in him purifies himself as he is pure. (1 John 3:2–3)

Change is not merely a matter of duty; it's a matter of vision. We *want* to be what we know we are ("God's children now") and one day will look like ("like him, because we shall see him as he is").

An American friend recently came to visit me in the UK. It was his first time outside the US, and he'd longed for many years to visit Britain. I spoke to him a couple of days before, and he was so excited that he was already trying to live in the UK time zone while still in Kentucky. This is someone who *hates* early starts, yet here he was trying to be dressed and in his right mind at four o'clock in the morning. Why? Because his heart was so fixed on where he was going. He wanted to do as much adjusting as he could before he even left.

So it is with us. The grace of God teaches us to say "No" to ungodliness and fires us up to live for Christ.

I'm sure that in years to come I'll look back on sermons I'm preaching now and still wince somewhat, just as I'll no doubt wince at my present clothing choices and hairstyle. It's a natural part of growth and development. With our preaching, we'll never fully arrive. Our sermons will never be perfect. Thankfully, they don't need to be.

My favorite castle, Bamburgh in Northumberland, sits atop a volcanic plug overlooking England's wild northeast coastline. Last summer as I walked along the vast beach, I noticed a sand castle made from a specially molded bucket so it had little turrets and battlements just like the real eleventh-century castle on the hill immediately behind it. I realized this is what preaching is like: trying with limited means to convey glories and beauties quite beyond our full grasp. I'll never do full justice to the biblical text, or to the Christ of whom it speaks. But not doing full justice is not the same as doing no justice at all. Our sermons will never be perfect. But, by God's grace, they don't need to be. Ultimately our prayer is that it will be Jesus himself who is preaching Sunday by Sunday. And *his* preaching is always perfect!

Discussion Questions

1. As you read chapter 5, what was the one insight that stood out to you most, and why?

2. It is often easier to preach the challenges of the law than it is to preach the peace of the gospel. The message of peace that comes down from God keeps surprising us all. Why is that so?

3. As we revel in what we now have in the new covenant, how can we ensure that in our preaching, the gospel itself is what's changing people?

Making Burdens Light

Ray: How can the ministry of preaching simultaneously announce gospel doctrine and nurture gospel culture? Let me pose two suggestions, Sam: the message and the tone.

In Matthew 11:30, Jesus says, "My yoke is easy, and my burden is light." I think that's the best hermeneutic with which to read the Bible from cover to cover, and the best message to convey wherever we are from Genesis to Revelation. Each passage will take us to Jesus from a different angle. Each one will show us something more about him, but each one will lead us into the light burden of his grace.

Don't misunderstand. Not every passage will be deeply comforting. There are unsettling passages in the Bible. When you're preaching through a book of the Bible and you come to an unsettling passage, let it be unsettling. Don't muffle the voice of that passage. But preach Christ through the passage. That's the difference between preaching and mere teaching.

Preaching is a personal invitation. It's not "Come and learn about Jesus." It's Jesus himself, through the preacher, saying, "Come to me."

Sam: I think it was Martyn Lloyd-Jones who said that he wanted people to stop taking notes in the last part of his sermon. If they were still taking notes, he regarded himself to have failed. He wanted people to be so focused on Jesus, so conscious of the presence of Jesus, that they weren't now thinking, "Oh, I need to write this down." They were just too in the moment. I love that aspiration.

Ray: Yes, with gospel preaching we all get reenergized, and less despairing, more hopeful in Jesus himself. It's not just instructional, it's alluring. I was with Willie Mackenzie in the Highlands of Scotland a few years ago, and he told me about an ordination exam where John Murray of Westminster Theological Seminary was one of the examiners. Murray asked the prospective minister, "What is the difference between preaching and teaching?" The young man didn't have a clear answer.

Murray proposed three Ps: personal, passionate, and pleading. When a pastor is preaching the Bible expositionally, the whole message funnels down to the all-sufficient grace of Christ for the undeserving. In his own authentic, nonweird, socially acceptable way in his cultural context, that pastor wants to reach out to the very hearts of the people with personal, passionate pleading. He opens the door for people to close with Christ, whether for the very first time or at their personal point of need that day. He leads them to take the outstretched hand of Christ in their own hand.

6

Leave Behind Lord-It-Over Leadership

A Culture Guided by Gentle Shepherds

You know that those who are considered rulers of the Gentiles lord it over them, and their great ones exercise authority over them. But it shall not be so among you.

MARK 10:42–43

THE VERSES PRINTED ABOVE from Mark 10 are the Bible's most significant statement on leadership. This passage may also be one of the most neglected among us.

Jesus starts with an observation. Leadership in the world around us is characterized by "lord[ing] it over" others (Mark 10:42). It's the default setting for human beings who have power—to put people in their place, to pull rank, to dominate, to rule the roost.

The evidence is all around us, in every sphere of life. Jesus says "you know" this. It's common knowledge. From prime ministers to parking lot attendants, give someone even a small amount of power, and they'll find a way to assert themselves over those who lack it. It's how the world works.

But Jesus says, "It shall not be so among you" (10:43).

Leadership in the church is to be fundamentally different from leadership in the world. The characteristics so visible in this world's rulers are to have no place among Jesus's people. Jesus himself shows us that greatness is not to be measured by prowess but service, not by following the examples of the world but by imitating the Savior before us, not by being served but by serving others.

Jesus's instruction about leadership has come up because of James and John. They'd just said to Jesus, "We want you to do for us whatever we ask of you" (10:35). It was hardly a great place to start. But before we too quickly judge them, we should recognize something of their attitude in our own hearts. We pastors have the capacity to view Jesus as a way to further our own agenda.

James and John's agenda was clear: "Grant us to sit, one at your right hand and one at your left, in your glory" (10:37). They had some notion Jesus was soon to come into glory. They'd misunderstood much of what Jesus had repeatedly taught about his forthcoming death and resurrection, but they'd at least picked up some sense that he would soon establish his rule. So, they wanted the two most prominent positions in that new order, to sit at either side of him. In today's terms, it was like requesting the two best roles in his cabinet. Their plan for Jesus was to make them great. We should see ourselves in that desire. Jesus immediately turns this into a lesson for *all* his followers, and this suggests we're fooling ourselves if we think we're above James and John's ambitions. After all, the way of the whole world is to measure greatness by power over others.

Leadership That Only Takes

The Bible illustrates this reality in Israel's own life. Saul's reign was paradigmatic of the very lord-it-over-them dynamic Jesus would later talk about. Israel had requested the kind of leader everyone else had: "a king to judge us *like all the nations*" (1 Sam. 8:5). God's response was to show Samuel that by making this request, "they [Israel] have rejected me from being king over them" (8:7). Seeking worldly leadership is not just unwise; it's spiritual rebellion.

God gives Israel what they asked, but he also warns them about the dark side of worldly kingship. One feature dominates:

> These will be the ways of the king who will reign over you: *he will take* your sons. . . . *He will take* your daughters. . . . *He will take* the best of your fields. . . . *He will take* the tenth of your grain and of your vineyards. . . . *He will take* your male servants and female servants and the best of your young men and your donkeys. . . . *He will take* the tenth of your flocks, and you shall be his slaves. And in that day you will cry out because of your king. (1 Sam. 8:11–18)

This is the end point of Gentile-style (a.k.a. human) leadership. The ruler *takes* and *takes*, and his people end up enslaved and crying out. As Jesus says, the rulers "lord it over them."

Whenever future generations of leaders in Israel gave into a lord-it-over-them dynamic, this provoked God to rebuke them:

Thus says the Lord God: Ah, shepherds of Israel who have been feeding yourselves! Should not shepherds feed the sheep? You eat the fat, you clothe yourselves with the wool, you slaughter the fat ones, but you do not feed the sheep. The weak you have not strengthened, the sick you have not healed, the injured you have not bound up, the strayed you have not brought back, the lost you have not sought, and with force and harshness you have ruled them. So they were scattered, because there was no shepherd, and they became food for all the wild beasts. My sheep were scattered; they wandered over all the mountains and on every high hill. My sheep were scattered over all the face of the earth, with none to search or seek for them. (Ezek. 34:2–6)

This is uncomfortable reading. God calls out the leaders for what they were *doing*: feeding and clothing themselves, seemingly taking all they could from the people, even destroying some of them. He also calls them out for what they *weren't* doing: they didn't strengthen, heal, and bind up the broken. They didn't seek the lost and strayed. They weren't just negligent, but destructive. So, God's people were scattered, lost, injured, and starved.

What was God's verdict? "I am against the shepherds," he says (34:10). God will put up with their failed leadership no longer.

Leadership that only takes is an ever-present danger. Ezekiel's false shepherds exploited the people. King Saul took for himself. This is the direction James and John were trending as well. They asked for prominence and power over others. Why? For what they'd get out of it. We mustn't think this is no temptation for us.

We've seen too many examples of calloused leadership in our churches in recent years. Some have been dramatic enough to make the headlines—megachurches and whole movements imploding as their leaders are exposed to be deceitful or abusive bullies. But there are many other examples on a smaller, less obvious scale. Lording it over others is a heart issue for every leader, and we mustn't think that just because we've not gone as far as the notorious offenders that we've somehow avoided the dangers.

The Danger of Worldly Models[1]

The church is many things at once. It's an edifice (1 Pet. 2:5) that requires systems, rosters, and programs. It is a body (Eph. 4:16), a complex whole with a variety and diversity of parts with each making a unique contribution. The church is a family (1 Tim. 3:15). It's not meant to be a place of impersonal efficiency but of highly relational care and consideration. It's an army engaged in a grueling campaign that requires focus and discipline (2 Cor. 10:3–5; 2 Tim. 2:3–4; Eph. 6:11–18). It's also a bride, pledged to her groom in holiness and devotion (2 Cor. 11:2). This multifaceted-ness of the church makes leading it a complex affair.

As such, it's inevitable that Christians will adopt models of leadership from our surrounding culture. Common grace means there will always be things we can learn about leadership from the world. There is wisdom to draw on from politics, business, and even the military. Pastors *may* glean leadership lessons from people as varied as Winston Churchill, Abraham Lincoln, Steve

---

1   Content in this section and the next is adapted from Sam Allberry, "How Do Churches End Up with Domineering Bullies for Pastors?" The Gospel Coalition (website), January 21, 2019, https://www.thegospelcoalition.org/.

Jobs, General B. L. Montgomery, Martin Luther King Jr., and Nelson Mandela.

But Jesus's observation about the "rulers of the Gentiles" (Mark 10:42) means we need to be extremely careful. Behind the good that can be learned from the world, there will also be underlying assumptions and trains of thought we must avoid. "It shall not be so among you" means there's to be a clear distinction between how leadership is exercised in the world and in the church. We can't just take concepts of leadership from the world around us, attempt to point them in a Christian direction, and think thereby our leadership is *Christian*.

In the US, I (Sam) have seen churches (and other Christian institutions, for that matter) where the leader and his wife are referred to and treated as the "first family," often with a measure of unhealthy excess and deference that the title implies. One would find it hard to imagine a pastor with this mindset embracing the suffering and humiliation Paul considered normative for Christian ministry (2 Cor. 11:23–29).

Another common trend is to see the pastor as CEO. His role is to bring "success," which is often measured in numerical terms through growth in membership, facilities, and giving. The pastor-as-CEO approach might foster entrepreneurialism and risk-taking, but it easily becomes results oriented. It can lead to swagger, arrogance, and a culture in which the pastor is seen as economically indispensable and above questioning.

In the UK, the church tends to draw leadership wisdom from boarding school and military contexts. This is unsurprising, given the influence that class has had on many parts of the British church. In this context, the pastor is less of a CEO and more of a general. He's the one who knows the battle plan and where everyone fits in. This mentality easily leads to aloofness and stoicism, with the pastor being emotionally above it all. It's hard for a pastor with this mindset to say with Paul, "For God is my witness, how I yearn for you all with the affection of Christ Jesus" (Phil. 1:8), or "Being affectionately desirous of you, we were ready to share with you not only the gospel of God but also our own selves, because you had become very dear to us" (1 Thess. 2:8). Instead, it's easy for a ministry with a military mindset to be defined by hierarchy and who's in charge.

I think of a respected British pastor—evidently quite the squash player—who put prospective and aspiring church staff "in their place" by roundly defeating them at squash. The game was used to establish beyond question that he was the one with power. I bring this up not because it's a dramatic example but because it's not uncommon among churches I've seen to have unwritten and unspoken initiations that domineering pastors put others through before they'll trust them. I came across a summer camp ministry, for example, whose policy was to never thank the team of volunteers whose sole role on the camp staff was to undertake menial tasks like setting up rooms, cleaning, and washing up after meals. The reason given was that these helpers needed to be kept humble.

But it's the very mindset of lording it over that Jesus forbids in Mark 10. Inasmuch as we're to put others "in their place," it should be to put them *above* us, not beneath us. As Christian leaders, we must establish that we're the servants and our role is to put others' needs and dignity before our own. There are dozens of "one another" verses in the New Testament, but none of them tells us to *humble* one another. The only person we're to humble is ourselves (1 Pet. 5:6).[2]

Shepherd the Flock without Domineering

Yes, we can learn from CEOs, generals, and many other leaders. But pastors are not meant to be CEOs and generals. As Peter makes clear, we are not to be domineering in ministry:

> So I exhort the elders among you, as a fellow elder and a witness of the sufferings of Christ, as well as a partaker in the glory that is going to be revealed: shepherd the flock of God that is among you, exercising oversight, not under compulsion, but willingly, as God would have you; not for shameful gain, but eagerly; not domineering over those in your charge, but being examples to the flock. (1 Pet. 5:1–3)

Peter draws three contrasts about the work and heart of an elder: (1) he must be willing, not coerced; (2) he must serve, not be greedy; and (3) he must lead by example, not by compulsion.

It's that final contrast that relates directly to Jesus's instruction in Mark 10. It's possible to use hierarchy and position to dominate others—for the flock to assent by compulsion rather than by the Spirit's work in their hearts. Such leadership involves the use of intimidation, coercion, threats, and bullying.

When Peter forbids domineering coercion, there may also be some connection with the previous contrasts he's just made: being domineering can be a form of "shameful gain"—that is, greed for

---

2 I'm grateful to my friend Jordan Thyer for this observation.

power over others. And if an elder must serve willingly (5:2), so too the flock must follow willingly. Peter's point is that domineering ministry is catastrophic. It may seem effective in the short term (It gets things done!), but it's disastrous in the long term.

What Paul says to the Romans about dealing with those "weak in faith" is instructive here (Rom. 14:1). Those weak in faith abstain from certain foods or observe certain days, though God doesn't require them to. Paul tells the church that if this has become a matter of conscience, they shouldn't be coerced into changing their practice: "Whoever has doubts is condemned if he eats, because the eating is not from faith. For whatever does not proceed from faith is sin" (Rom. 14:23). Here Paul highlights a broad principle that applies beyond the immediate discussion about food and special days. *Whatever* doesn't proceed from faith is sin. If a believer has certain doctrinal views or behaves in certain ways simply because a pastor has coerced such behavior, then those views or actions do not proceed from faith. It's not the Spirit of Christ who has brought them about but the forcefulness of the leader. This is catastrophic because such a believer isn't led by the Lord, but by man. Saying or doing the right things is no good if one's conscience and relationship with God are damaged in the process.

True Greatness of the Good Shepherd

Jesus is clear that we're meant to be serving, not lording it over, those in our churches:

> But whoever would be great among you must be your servant, and whoever would be first among you must be slave of all.

For even the Son of Man came not to be served but to serve, and to give his life as a ransom for many. (Mark 10:43–45)

Greatness, in Jesus's eyes, is not measured by how many people are under us but by how many people we regard as being above us. If the one we'd most expect to have the world revolving around him—namely, the Son of Man—is content to take the role of a servant, then we who are far less worthy than he is have even more reason to take that role. When we put others below us, we risk putting ourselves not just over them but over Jesus too.

Think back to the shameful leaders of Ezekiel's day. God not only exposes their wickedness but outlines what's to be done. He will remove them and—astonishingly—replace them with himself: "Behold, I, I myself will search for my sheep and will seek them out" (Ezek. 34:11). God is saying that they don't need a better system. They need a better shepherd. So, God will attend to them personally. He will gather them (34:12–13), care for them (34:14–16), and provide justice (34:16–19). He will be all the leader they need.

This promise, of course, is fulfilled in Jesus's coming. He's the good shepherd foretold in Ezekiel. It's his presence as the perfect leader of God's people that is the answer to the wrong thinking about leadership we can so easily slip into.

Recognizing the good shepherd provides us with three foundational truths for leadership:

First, the sheep are God's. Within God's rebuke of the wicked shepherds in Ezekiel 34, we see a shift take place. After talking about *the* sheep in 34:1–4, he begins to call them *my* sheep in 34:5 and continues to do so through the rest of the passage. Those under a pastor's leadership are not his but God's. Recognizing this is foundational to healthy ministry. The church is not the pastor's but God's. It might be convenient shorthand to refer to a particular church as "Pastor So-and-so's church," but it can be an unhealthy habit to get into. Every single believer we encounter is someone who belongs to God above.

Paul was aware of this reality when he said to the Ephesian elders, "Pay careful attention to yourselves and to all the flock, in which the Holy Spirit has made you overseers, to care for the church of God, which he obtained with his own blood" (Acts 20:28). Paul stresses not just God's ownership of the flock but the unimaginable price by which he obtained it—his own blood. The church body is God's, and it's inestimably precious to him. Such a thought should stop us in our tracks.

It's not surprising that Paul also recognizes that ministry itself is God's: "If only I may finish my course and the ministry that I received from the Lord Jesus" (20:24). Again, we need to be careful with our language. It may not be healthy for us to think in terms of "our" or "my" ministry. The work is the Lord's. It's his gospel, his church, his world.

Over four billion viewers were estimated to have watched the funeral of Queen Elizabeth, and I was among them. As the pallbearers lifted her coffin onto their shoulders at the end of the service, it occurred to me how terrifying that could've been. Doing anything in front of a global audience of that size is intimidating enough, but they hoisted up not only the late monarch but the imperial crown, orb, and scepter. It's hard to imagine a more valuable load to carry. But surely that's only a fraction of how precious the flock is that pastors care for and carry. It is, as Paul says elsewhere, a noble task to which to aspire (1 Tim. 3:1). But it is also, understandably, not one to presume upon (James 3:1).

Second, pastors are but undershepherds. If Jesus is the good shepherd, that means church leaders are his very, very junior colleagues. Peter calls church leaders to "shepherd the flock of God that is among you" while also reminding them that "the chief Shepherd" himself will one day appear (1 Pet. 5:2–4). A church leader's pastoral authority isn't ultimate. The pastor is there to serve under the real Shepherd. Whatever the church's organizational chart may say, Jesus himself is the congregation's lead pastor.

This is humbling, but it's also reassuring. If God himself is the ultimate shepherd, I can breathe. I have responsibility—sobering responsibility—but God has the ultimate responsibility. I can do no better as a pastor than to lead the sheep to Jesus's voice. When I bring people to *his* word to be led by *him*, I can rest assured I'm being faithful.

A significant part of that faithfulness is being careful to make sure my own leadership reflects his own. If Jesus is the good shepherd, we undershepherds have a responsibility to lead as much as possible in a way that points to his own shepherding heart, in a way that makes it obvious what kind of shepherd he is. Faithfulness is not just a matter of having the right content in our teaching but the right posture and tone and demeanor too. We should make it easier for the sheep to believe that the *chief* shepherd really is the *good* shepherd.

Dane Ortlund's book *Gentle and Lowly: The Heart of Christ for Sinners and Sufferers* has had a significant impact since its release in 2020, both in how widely read it has become and (more importantly) in how it has awakened so many to Christ's character.

The fact that Jesus is indeed gentle and lowly in heart seems to have been a revelation to many and a huge relief to many more. But this raises an uncomfortable question: Could it be that all this time we pastors have not been shepherding in a way that made it obvious that Jesus is gentle? Whatever else the pastor's responsibilities may be, he is a reference point for what Jesus is like. People's deepest impression of who Christ is will inevitably come from what they perceive their pastor's heart toward them is. So, is the book our hearts are publishing entitled *Gentle and Lowly*, or is it *Demanding and Aloof* or *Irritable and Exasperated*?

Third, the pastor is both a shepherd and a sheep. He's a member of the very flock he serves. Unlike regular shepherds, he's not a different species from the sheep and detached from them; he's one of them.

This reality is reflected in much of the New Testament's language about elders. Though the pastor is set over the flock (1 Thess. 5:12), that isn't his only relationship to it. Peter writes, "Shepherd the flock of God that is *among* you" (1 Pet. 5:2). This flock is not only *under you* but *among you*. As the pastor, you are both *over* the people and *with* them.

Because the pastor is also a sheep, he too is on the path of growth. Paul therefore says to Timothy,

Do not neglect the gift you have, which was given you by prophecy when the council of elders laid their hands on you. Practice these things, immerse yourself in them, so that all may see your progress. (1 Tim. 4:14–15)

Timothy still has progress to make. Even the apostle must say, "Not that I have already obtained this or am already perfect, but

I press on to make it my own" (Phil. 3:12). Paul had more to obtain, further distance to cover on the way to perfection, and so he was in an ongoing process of pressing on. All true disciples are aware of how much further they must go—pastors, no less so.

Example of Progress

Paul shows us that the ongoing growth of the pastor isn't to be hidden from the church's view. They need to see it. They must know the pastor himself is a work in progress and not the finished product or final authority. He's learning, growing, and developing in both life and doctrine.

This means the pastor must demonstrate ongoing repentance, for no Christian grows without repentance. There will be sins the pastor becomes convicted of—truths he now realizes he'd either misunderstood, wrongly emphasized, or neglected. There are appropriate ways to reflect this before the church. Indeed, it's healthy to do so. A pastor I know once confessed in a sermon how irritable he'd been driving on the way to church that morning. He'd felt convicted of it by the text he was preaching. Another pastor—a single man at the time—confessed that when his friend had sex before marriage, he'd felt both brokenhearted for the friend but also a little jealous. In each case, the admissions were appropriate, given what was being preached and in how they were expressed.

There will be times pastors need to apologize to members of the church, even to the church itself. It hurts one's ego to confess sin publicly, but it reassures the church that their pastor is a real Christian and that he, like them, is striving to put sin to death and press on in holiness. Knowing he too is flesh and blood also makes it a little easier for others to move forward in their own confession and repentance.

The pastor's example—not of perfection, but of progress— is what Peter points to as the antidote to domineering ministry (1 Pet. 5:3). What should make a pastor compelling to the flock is not the force of his personality but the genuineness of his example. That will be a more powerfully energizing force in the church than force or control. That will be what truly changes lives.

Indeed, this is part of the point Jesus is making in Mark 10: "You know that those who are *considered* rulers of the Gentiles lord it over them, and their great ones exercise authority over them" (10:42). Jesus call them not just *rulers* of the Gentiles but those who are *considered* rulers of the Gentiles. They seem to be shaping the course of history. But they have only an appearance of power and significance. They're *considered* rulers, but there is in fact a far more potent force at work in the world than that wielded by prime ministers and presidents. It's why Jesus goes on to say,

> Whoever would be great among you must be your servant, and whoever would be first among you must be slave of all. For even the Son of Man came not to be served but to serve, and to give his life as a ransom for many. (10:43–45)

Lording it over people can certainly change people's behavior. But only the loving service of the Son of Man can truly change someone's heart. Greatness is doing all we can to emulate and reflect his heart to those entrusted to our care. When Jesus, our good shepherd, fills our horizon, self-importance will become ugly to us, and service and humility beautiful.

Discussion Questions

1. As you read chapter 6, what was the one insight that stood out to you most, and why?

2. What is it about worldly leadership in our churches that—let's be honest—sometimes appeals to us? *Why* do sincere Christians across the spectrum of our denominations lapse in this way?

3. How might you help your church move toward displaying the beauty of gentleness (Eph. 4:2) and reasonableness (Phil. 4:5) more and more? How can you do this in a way that is itself gentle and reasonable? In other words, how can you move toward change without making divisions worse?

But What about Our Divided Churches?

Sam: If God is in control, we don't have to be controlling.

Ray: We sure don't. In fact, as you've said, Sam, it's a gospel advantage *not* to be controlling. We have better things to do. Philippians 4:5 says, "Let your reasonableness [or *gentleness*, ESV margin note] be known to everyone. The Lord is at hand." The word here can mean noninsistent, yielding, gentle, kind, courteous, or tolerant behavior. This reasonableness makes allowances for people on disputed issues.

Of course, we don't condone sin. The Bible is clear about that. You and I, Sam, are men of theological conscience. We're men of conviction and principle. When we talk about gentleness, we're not out to distort righteousness or draw the lines in the wrong place. We call sin "sin" because we're biblical men. But a culture of gentle leadership means that people who differ on serious issues can belong together in the same church. Our own church, for instance, has both Republicans and Democrats. We make room for one another.

Sam: I wonder whether part of why we're able to do that—to have people come to different political conclusions—is because of the reasonableness Philippians 4:5 talks about. Christians in our church have tried to think through their politics Christianly, with a good conscience, and they've come to conclusions different from what you or I might have. So, I wonder whether part of the reasonableness isn't simply looking at where someone is and saying, "I think you're wrong on that," but, "I can see how you've gotten there, . . ."

Ray: Oh, that's good.

Sam: ". . . and I can honor how you've gotten there, even if it's not the same conclusion I've come to. I can honor the process by which you've arrived at your conclusions." That's the kind of reasonable approach we should have in the case of all sorts of issues the Bible calls disputable. Such a case includes someone's understanding of baptism or the Lord's return. I'm less interested in what they think. I'm more interested in the reasonableness with which they got there.

Ray: When we're reasonable, we're showing that gospel doctrine has created a gospel culture. And we're not just a new community; we're a new *kind* of community—a community of gentle reasonableness, where "the Lord is at hand" (Phil. 4:5).

7

Make Your Church's
Love Obvious

A Culture Fueled by Renewal and Mission

By this all people will know that you are my
disciples, if you have love for one another.

JOHN 13:35

GIVING PASTORAL ATTENTION to the healthy, familial life of
a church does not distract from evangelism. We might think it
does. Some might say it does. After all, our churches have limited
resources and energy. We could expend endless energy nurturing
community inside our churches and neglect urgent spiritual needs
outside our churches. Surely it is better to focus our finite effort
on what is most urgent, right?

The New Testament offers us wiser categories of understanding. If we put mission front and center with community only

as a time-permitting afterthought, we'll discover we are not only less compelling as a community but also less convincing in our attempts to reach the world. Jesus himself brings us into a new kind of community with one another. He died to do so. And it's this kind of community life that empowers the church's mission.

What we are saying in this book is basically this: *Gospel doctrine, when we pastors allow it to exert its true authority, leads to gospel culture.* Now, this chapter is our final step together. And here's what we're saying: *gospel culture energizes the church's mission to the world.*

Jesus and Community

In Mark 10, Jesus gives us this staggering promise:

> Jesus said, "Truly, I say to you, there is no one who has left house or brothers or sisters or mother or father or children or lands, for my sake and for the gospel, who will not receive a hundredfold now in this time, houses and brothers and sisters and mothers and children and lands, with persecutions, and in the age to come eternal life." (Mark 10:29–30)

What we leave. Jesus is always honest, even blunt, about the cost of discipleship. He never buries suffering in the small print. He wants us to know that following him will be hard.

Here he takes it for granted we'll leave dear things and people behind to follow him. The fact is, we can't turn *to* him without also turning *from* other things. All Christians bear some cost in following Jesus, though we may not always see it. Rosaria Butterfield once said, "We may never know the treacherous journey people have taken to land in the pew next to us."[1] It's one of the reasons we need to go easy on each other; we just don't see all people are going through. We don't see the price they may be paying just to show up at church.

Jesus knows that the costliest things to leave will be relational. He foresees believers losing their kin, their homes, their very sense of belonging to follow him. Thankfully, that's not the case for many of us, but there will be some from certain backgrounds for whom allegiance to Jesus will mean they're no longer welcome in their community. Yet even when the cost is so high, Jesus assures us he's worth it.

This should never cease to amaze us. The instinct of so many is to feel that nothing is more important than family. Even in the West, we still think this way. But along comes Jesus, and quite unselfconsciously says "I am" (see John 8:48, for example). He audaciously claims to supersede the most significant human relationships we have in this life. He eclipses all others. He assumes he's more compelling than all of them, even all of them combined. We're used to the deep bonds of loyalty that exist in many families, and to the intoxication that overwhelms young lovers. But Jesus says he exceeds both, that he is more captivating, enthralling, and *urgent* than all others. Having all the friendship, family, and romantic fulfillment we could possibly imagine and desire without Jesus would not be worth it.

1   Rosaria Butterfield, "Homosexuality and the Christian Faith." Breakout talk given at The Gospel Coalition's 2014 National Women's Conference, June 29, 2014. Available online at https://www.thegospelcoalition.org/conference_media/homosexuality -christian-faith/.

What we receive. But when we follow Jesus, we don't just get Jesus on his own. Whatever relational cost following Jesus might incur, he also wants us to know that following him is worth it in this life, not just in the age to come. Even in the present age, we'll receive back from Jesus far, far more than we leave behind. The hardest cost for following Jesus is familial and relational, but, in a similar way, it's familial and relational blessings that he promises us.

You will have houses: homes in which you're welcome, places where people truly get you, where you feel most understood. Lands where you deeply feel you belong. You'll have family: people who are given to you as fathers and mothers, brothers and sisters, sons and daughters. And lest his promises sound utterly idealized, there will be a side order of persecutions too—whether or not we ordered them.

It's hard to overstate the grandeur of what Jesus is saying here. Whatever is to our relational loss in coming to Jesus and following him will be made up for by a couple orders of magnitude. Jesus promises that with him we'll never be relationally out of pocket. He's not even promising that whatever we lose, he'll give us a bit more; he's promising us *a hundredfold return!*

Jesus doesn't promise health and wealth. He doesn't promise a life without hardship where everything only gets better and easier. He *does* promise deep and rich community, the likes of which we'd never have without him.

A friend of mine (Sam's) came to faith from a Muslim background. He knew he'd most likely be rejected by his family if he became a Christian. It's a horrific cost, unimaginable to so many of us. But think about what Jesus promises my friend: more community and family than he had before, not less. This doesn't mean the pain of what he lost would easily go away, but it does mean that alongside that painful loss is a hundredfold gain.

Let us marvel at the generous provision of Christ. He cares about this side of life. Having thick community matters to him. He wants us to have people to be friends with and to do life with, and he wants it so much he promises to provide it. By promising it so explicitly and emphatically, Jesus is staking his reputation here. If his promise isn't true, then Jesus isn't true. But we mustn't miss the implications for us and our churches. We're not bystanders, passively looking on as Jesus makes this promise to abandoned disciples. We are not only the people to whom the promise is made (inasmuch as the gospel has had relational cost in our own lives). No, we are the fathers and mothers, brothers and sisters, sons and daughters Jesus promises.

What we provide. Often Jesus's promises are such that only he can fulfill them. When he promises the thief on the cross, "Today you will be with me in paradise" (Luke 23:43), or says, "Whoever comes to me I will never cast out" (John 6:37), we don't roll up our sleeves to help out. These are things only Jesus can accomplish, commitments only he can fulfill.

But the promise in Mark 10 is different. We are the hundredfold blessing he promises.

Jesus offers our homes and lands to others. In J. R. R. Tolkien's *The Hobbit*, a succession of dwarfs interrupts Bilbo Baggins's domestic peace and tranquility. The dwarfs presume they can avail themselves of his food and hospitality. As the story unfolds, it emerges that the wizard Gandalf, without seeking Bilbo's prior approval, had scratched a magic invitation for the dwarfs on the hobbit's front door![2]

Jesus does something very similar to our homes. If we're his disciples, the places where we dwell are no longer exclusively ours. We're to share them with those to whom Jesus makes this Mark 10 promise. We must be willing for others to barge in and help themselves to the contents of our pantry. He has promised *them* our home and land.

Let's not congratulate ourselves on being philanthropic. Jesus's call means we will need to move beyond our comfort levels. Something in us will be diminished if we don't. But it isn't just what we have. It's who we are that is bound up in his promise. Jesus offers *us* to others. He mentions three generations: the one going before us (*mothers and fathers*), our own (*brothers and sisters*), and the one ahead (*children*). To each we are to be family.

Thinking of the generation that has come before us, we're to ask, Who can we be a son or daughter to? Who can we look up to and learn from? Who will have more wisdom than us about life in God's world? Of our own generation, Who could we walk alongside as a Christian brother or sister? Who can we encourage and be encouraged by? And of the generation ahead of us, Who is there we have some wisdom to share with? Who could we be a spiritual father or mother to?

Church as Family

How wonderful that every one of us can do something, no matter what our age and Christian experience. For pretty much all of

---

2 I'm grateful to Pastor T. J. Tims for this analogy.

us, there will be people before, alongside, or coming ahead that we can be family to.

We see this vision reflected in these words of Paul to Timothy: "Do not rebuke an older man but encourage him as you would a father, younger men as brothers, older women as mothers, younger women as sisters, in all purity" (1 Tim. 5:1–2). Timothy is to treat the church as family, as an immediate and close family. Older men and women are not just to be treated as uncles and aunts but as fathers and mothers, younger men and women not just as distant cousins but as brothers and sisters.

Strikingly, Paul's language recognizes the reality of both age and biological sex as theologically significant. Fathers and mothers are not identical or interchangeable. The way Timothy is to relate to them is different. The same is the case with brothers and sisters. Paul is assuming that healthy behavior to brothers and sisters will look slightly different. Timothy isn't to withdraw from relationship with his Christian sisters, but he is to relate to them with purity.

It's not just our biological sex that is theologically significant; so is our age. Timothy is to treat older men in a way that is slightly different from how he is to treat younger men, and from how he relates to older women and younger women. You are not simply as old as you feel. You are as old as you are, and it's part of your God-given embodied life in this world. These are realities we mustn't deny and must in fact honor.

Our culture tends to demean old age while revering youth, attractiveness, and with-it-ness. Sometimes we see this in churches too where the emphasis often falls on children's or youth ministry as if it's assumed these are of greater intrinsic value. I don't think

I've ever seen a church advertise its thriving ministry to the elderly. But the Bible gives us a very different perspective:

> Wisdom is with the aged,
>   and understanding in length of days. (Job 12:12)

> The glory of young men is their strength,
>   but the splendor of old men is their gray hair.
>   (Prov. 20:29)

> You shall stand up before the gray head and honor the face of an old man, and you shall fear your God: I am the Lord. (Lev. 19:32)

As someone with rapidly graying hair, I can appreciate these verses. But the real point is that age is valued as being a form of spiritual capital and a blessing to the church, not a hindrance. Our older brothers and sisters represent the church's wisdom. A genuine gospel community will celebrate this.

These Scripture passages on the church as a spiritual family in no way obliterate our existing biological family structures and the obligations that come with them. Jesus and Paul aren't replacing the nuclear family. They are enriching the church family. They have an expansive understanding of "family" such that our commitments to our biological family should be honored alongside our commitments to our church family.

This matters because our church family is what is included in Jesus's promise. He promised an abundance of family to those who bear the heaviest relational cost of following him. If we don't attend to living as that family, we risk making Jesus look like a liar. The relational health of the local church is not incidental. It must not be an afterthought because his reputation is on the line.

But if we do live together in our churches as spiritual family, our churches become living proof of how following Jesus really is worth it. They shine forth a reality that a watching world can't fail to see.

Community and Mission

A church is not just a truth-dispensing center but a spiritual family. As Paul explains why he's written his first letter to Timothy, he provides this theologically concentrated definition of the church: "If I delay, you may know how one ought to behave in *the household of God*, which is the church *of the living God, a pillar and buttress of the truth*" (1 Tim. 3:15).

A friend of mine was walking past a church as its service was concluding. As the people poured out of the building, he noticed that none of them were talking together. There were no conversations. Whatever this congregation had come for, they'd come for it individually, and they'd gotten it, and now they were leaving. The presence of the rest of the congregation was apparently incidental. Sadly, it appeared to be a privatized spirituality. But that's not the spirituality of the New Testament. The church is the *household of God*, so we can expect relationships, interaction, and shared identity to be fundamental aspects of its life. Moreover, because this is the church *of the living God*, we can expect the family dynamics of this community to be energized by the life of God himself.

This is relevant given the final definition of a church in these verses. Paul goes on to say that the church is *the pillar and buttress of the truth*. Pillars and buttresses support large buildings. On vacation last summer, I visited Palma Cathedral on the Spanish island of Mallorca. It's one of the largest Gothic cathedrals in the world, and it has beautiful pillars and buttresses. They're essential for a building of its size and dimensions, but they aren't just functional, they're ornate. They're part of the beauty of the building they support.

A church is to be the same for God's truth. It is not that the truth needs a church's stamp of approval. Nor is it simply that a church is the outlet for God's truth in the world (though that is true). Far more, a church validates and embodies God's truth in the world. The beauty of community in a church is meant to be a plausibility structure for the gospel, lifting its social visibility as a pillar, reinforcing its persuasive power as a buttress. A church makes the gospel known and even compelling. And it will not be a captivating voice for the truth if it is not living as a beautiful family.

Jesus himself shows us this when he says, "By this all people will know that you are my disciples, if you have love for one another" (John 13:35). If we didn't already know how it ended, we might instinctively complete this sentence differently. In our heart of hearts, we sometimes believe the world will know we're Jesus's disciples if we're more impressive than our surrounding culture, if we have a mic-drop answer to every skeptic's question, if our people seem more put together than everyone else, or if our preacher is always telegenic and our music team always gives a virtuoso performance.

But Jesus puts his emphasis elsewhere. What will most clearly show the presence of heaven on earth—that God is alive and well and *right here*—is our *love* for one another. Our shared love is not an afterthought, as though what really mattered were these other things and our love for one another was added as a bonus. No, the quality of our relational life in our churches is to be an apologetic for the world around us. As Francis Schaeffer once wrote, "Jesus is giving the world permission to judge whether we are true Christian disciples on the basis of whether we love one another."[3]

Jesus expresses a similar idea in his prayer just a few hours later:

The glory that you have given me I have given to them, that they may be one even as we are one, I in them and you in me, that they may become perfectly one, so that the world may know that you sent me and loved them even as you loved me. (John 17:22–23)

This is a sacred moment. We are listening in to the eternal Son as he prays to the eternal Father. He prays for us. We are the "them" to whom Jesus refers. We are those who would come to believe through his apostles' message. And what does Jesus pray for? He prays for our unity, praying that the oneness he and the Father share will mark his people as well, that we would "become perfectly one."

What's astonishing is the impact Jesus prays our loving unity will have. He's not praying for our sakes alone. No, Jesus prays for our unity "so that the world may know that you sent me and loved them even as you loved me." In our love for one another, the world around us is meant to see evidence that Jesus has been sent

3   Francis A. Schaeffer, *The Mark of the Christian* (Downers Grove, IL: InterVarsity Press, 1970), 27.

from heaven. They're meant to see that something of the eternal love that the Father has for the Son now rests on us.

Our love for one another is not only meant to be clearly observable by the watching world. It's to be so strikingly Godlike that it cannot be explained except by the reality of the gospel. The gospel doctrines of the incarnation ("you sent me") and of justification ("and loved them") will become more visible and nonignorable through the love we show one another in Christ.

Early Church Example

This isn't just theoretical or aspirational. We *see* this dynamic in the life of the early church. Look at their life together:

> And they devoted themselves to the apostles' teaching and the fellowship, to the breaking of bread and the prayers. And awe came upon every soul, and many wonders and signs were being done through the apostles. And all who believed were together and had all things in common. And they were selling their possessions and belongings and distributing the proceeds to all, as any had need. And day by day, attending the temple together and breaking bread in their homes, they received their food with glad and generous hearts, praising God and having favor with all the people. And the Lord added to their number day by day those who were being saved. (Acts 2:42–47)

Here we're given a snapshot of the early church's communal life. Luke writes of them being devoted not just to the apostles' teaching, vital though that was, but to *fellowship*. They were conscious of the stake they had in one another. Twice he mentions the *breaking of bread*, no doubt a reference to sharing the Lord's Supper, but just as certainly an indication that these believers also frequently shared meals together. They were in one another's *homes*. They *shared their possessions* with one another. They were familiar enough with one another's lives to know what needs there were, and they were close enough in heart to want to give materially to meet those needs. These people knew each other deeply. And Luke concludes, "The Lord added to their number day by day."

Interestingly, Luke doesn't say, "They were active in sharing their faith, and the church grew daily." It's not that there wasn't active evangelism going on. Luke gives us plenty of examples in the following chapters of Christians who proclaimed the gospel to the world around them (see Acts 8:4, for example). The New Testament is clear that Christians have a responsibility to share their faith (see Col. 4:6 and 1 Pet. 3:15). Luke's wording in Acts 2:47 offers no basis for denying the importance of evangelism.

But Luke's focus is significant. He wants us to see, first, that it's God who does the growing. The growth of the church isn't to be accounted for solely by human agency. God is the one adding to their number. God is the one who awakens people to faith in Christ. But, second, I suspect Luke wants us to see that the human agency most relevant to this growth is what he's just been describing in the previous verses—the early church's devotion to teaching, prayer, worship, and, not least, to one another. This kind of gospel community, with people praying, praising, eating, doing life with each other, and caring for one another in costly ways will be nonignorable to the world around. This kind of church will grow. Their life together drips with gospel truth.

Such a community will inevitably accelerate the church's mission. Love like this cannot fail to deeply affect those who look on.

Neptune was the first planet discovered by mathematics rather than observation.[4] It wasn't that someone chanced upon it while looking through a telescope one day. Rather, astronomers worked out that this planet must exist and even where it would be. In the 1840s, John Couch Adams and others had noticed various irregularities in the orbit of Uranus. It deviated significantly from its expected path. The only explanation was that there was something else out there, some other planetary body whose gravity was tugging away and causing Uranus to move out of its predicted orbit. Individuals like Adams were able to extrapolate from these irregularities exactly where this other planet must be without even seeing it. The existence and location of Neptune was a mathematical certainty before anyone set eyes on it.

A church, your church, is to be so marked by the love of Christ that his existence will be believed even when he himself isn't seen. We're to be gospel truth incarnated in gospel culture. Doctrinal beauty creating relational beauty. As the world looks on, they will see what appears to be all sorts of irregularities, deviations from the normal paths of behavior such as sins freely confessed, grace extended and received, people honored and encouraged, and the welcome of Christ made manifest through mutual care and embrace. As a result, the presence and smile of Jesus himself will become a felt human reality.

---

4 This paragraph and the two following are adapted from Sam Allberry, *Connected: Living in the Light of the Trinity* (Nottingham, UK: Inter-Varsity Press, 2012), 133–34. Used with permission.

Such wonders will be deeply curious irregularities to a watching world, lines of behavior that don't move in the directions people have come to expect. An orbit of life that is unmistakably different. Instances of deep love that reveal the gravitational pull of a greater and unseen presence. Undeniable signs that this community of believers is held together by nothing less than a divine love. The spectator who begins to ponder these earthbound irregularities will, by grace, be directed to the perfect heavenly source of them all.

Discussion Questions

1. As you read chapter 7, what was the one insight that stood out to you most, and why?

2. Loving community enhances missionality because community *is* missional. Why do we tend to separate the two in our churches? And how can we help our churches strengthen both?

3. Which aspect of our Lord's new commandment (John 13:34–35) is hardest for you? Is there a friend in your church with whom you can pray, asking the Lord for his love to go viral in your heart and church?

Putting the Emphasis in the Right Place

Ray: I'm looking right now at the membership directory—the photo directory—of a church I once pastored. It was a great privilege to serve them many years ago. I open the book to page 1, and the first thing that meets my eyes is the words "Our Ministry Emphases." We have the mission of the church stated there and subcategories: "The Worship of God, the Ministry of the Word, the Discipleship of the World." There are two things that bother me about that list now. First, I wish we'd put Jesus first before our ministry emphases. The first page in our church directory should have been our Savior. The other thing that bothers me is there's not a single reference to our being a family, to our being brothers and sisters in Christ who share mutual love, esteem, honesty, honor, and support. It's sad to me that, at the time, I didn't see that as a problem.

Sam: It's common for us to skip over community straight to mission, isn't it? But what we don't realize is that if we do, we're going to have a much less effective mission. The way God has designed his gospel to flourish is through the relational beauty of the church commending and confirming the message we preach. If we rush into mission as a bare task, a thing on its own, we won't have the same traction.

Ray: So what we're saying is, "Let's be self-aware about what we're prioritizing." We all want people to be evangelized, to be converted, to join the church, and to grow. But who in our city in their right minds would want to join our church? Why should anybody join? Why would any legitimately self-interested, self-motivated human being choose cheerfully to come join this Christian church? We must respect our communities enough to give them good answers to those questions. If the only answer is Jesus, who will forgive your sins and so forth, that's not a bad answer. But it's not the total answer Jesus himself gives. He did not come to save and redeem isolated individuals into a band of isolated individuals like pennies in a jar. He came to gather in his elect from all the nations so they might form a body, one that is joined together, lives together, and dies together. There's a quality of community with which people in your city and mine will see and resonate with. They'll say, "My life would get better if I were among those people."

Sam: Paul says in Ephesians 3:10 that it's through the church that the manifold wisdom of God is made known to the rulers and authorities in heavenly places. It is that new society God has created that blows a raspberry to the devil.

Ray: I like that. Sam, you're being charmingly British. I love that expression. I'm going to start using it.

Sam: Okay, well, let's start a campaign. If God really wants to stick it to the devil, he only needs to point to his church because there's a reality there that embodies the beauty and the supremacy and the triumph of Christ.

Ray: Sam, when you say that something inside you lights up, and it makes me think. I'm not willing to pray and suffer and labor and give my life to maintain an ecclesiastical institution that isn't beautiful. But I am willing to labor and suffer and pray for and give my life to the creation of a beautiful church that can astonish this generation. Sign me up for that. That's gospel culture.

Conclusion

Let love be genuine.

ROMANS 12:9

DISINGENUOUS LOVE is all around us in our world today.

There's the love that's only words. A friend of mine has never liked his stepfather, and the feeling is mutual. Yet whenever I hear them speak on the phone, they always end the conversation by saying "love you" to one another. It's not because they do; it's just how that family concludes phone calls. But the language of love is empty without the presence of love. In our churches, the Lord has called us to something beautiful and costly: "Let us not love in word or talk but in deed and truth" (1 John 3:18).

There's also the kind of love that's only actions. It's easy to think we're loving someone well if all we do is notice the good we do for them. But we can be spectacularly altruistic and yet devoid of genuine love: "If I give away all I have, and if I deliver up my body to be burned, but have not love, I gain nothing" (1 Cor. 13:3).

The *genuine* love our Lord calls us to is deeper than mere words or deeds. The apostle Paul writes, "Love one another with brotherly affection" (Rom. 12:10). Genuine love can and must be defined further. As this Scripture says, it's a matter of affection. It's deeply heartfelt. Jesus's presence in our lives is the death of indifference, the death of aloofness—concealed under nice words and impressive deeds. His gospel brings us alive to a new reality. We're bound together now. We're family. Jesus gets us thinking, "You're not just in my contacts, or on our church's membership list, but in my very heart. And I wouldn't *want* it any other way."

And isn't that heartfelt affection what we all want, way deep down? A church community beautified by genuine love will be safe. We won't have to brace ourselves before entering the church building. We'll be able to exhale, to relax and rethink our lives at a deep level. If the world around us sometimes injures us, like Frodo's stab by the Nazgul on Weathertop, the church is meant to be Rivendell, where we can recover and heal. It should be a *relief* to turn up each Sunday. When gospel doctrine really enters our hearts, that gospel culture springs to life!

Afterword

DEAR ONE,

If I had been given the opportunity, I would have loved to have been praying for you as you read and experienced the pages of this book, written by my two brothers in the faith, Ray and Sam. Please know that I love and respect them more than I can ever adequately communicate. After nearly forty years of ministry, I am more than aware of the many times I should have wished for someone to be praying for me as I encountered life- and ministry-changing truths in a book, a teaching, or a relationship.

Though I have left behind and repented for most of what I learned and taught during the secularized church growth movement of the later part of the twentieth century, one reality I now believe is that, indeed, *culture eats strategy for breakfast*. I said this glib phrase for years, but it was not until one day, in my study alone, that the Holy Spirit came and convicted me of its truth. In my ministry life, I had marched God's people through forty days of everything, done hundreds of "programs," and developed small group system after small group system, but none of this actually changed or altered the *culture* of the congregations of saints that I had led. It took me some time to come to terms with the fact that most of my ministry had been driven by strategy and not the cultivating of a culture. Sam and Ray have cast a vision of culture change for us, and I hope that you will hear the need to move from strategy to culture cultivation.

Now more than ever, I believe we are amid another reformation in the church. I sense another awakening of followers of Jesus throughout the world, coming to the Spirit-driven conviction that our communities of faith are being called to recalibrate our personal and corporate lives back to God's design, the design as he describes and lays out in his Scriptures. And this kind of reformation will lead to revival!

You might be tempted to read a book like this and say to yourself, "Well, that all goes without saying." Unfortunately, that which goes without saying ends up going without doing or living, and that which goes without living or doing ends up being empty and shallow and without the life-changing power God intended for our lives, our ministry, and our mission. Let God nurture in you the life and gospel truths you have encountered in these seven short chapters. Let him change the world again by starting with you and with me.

Though I was not able to pray for you as you read this book, please let me pray with you now:

Heavenly Father, in you alone do we live and move and have our being.

Look with favor upon these, your servants, as they contemplate and inwardly digest the truths just read. By the power of your Holy Spirit, come and give them a special benediction of your grace to take in the truth of this book. May it inspire the creation of a Christ-saturated culture and community over which they have responsibility. Inspire them with faith and creativity as to how they are to surrender their individual lives, those of their families, and those they are entrusted with spiritually to grow into the full maturity and love of Christ. And we ask this in the name of our Lord Jesus Christ, whom we worship and adore.

Clark Lowenfield

BISHOP, THE ANGLICAN DIOCESE OF THE WESTERN GULF COAST

THE ANGLICAN CHURCH OF NORTH AMERICA

Acknowledgments

WE STARTED OUR PODCAST, *You're Not Crazy*, in late 2021. The world was still reeling from the Covid-19 pandemic. Churches were reeling from the political divisions it had aroused. We hoped our conversations would encourage pastors and others who find their churches to be unusually weary. We were thinking especially of pastors in their early years of ministry.

Though the subtitle of the podcast is *Gospel Sanity for Young Pastors*, we've been surprised at how the Lord has used it among many who aren't pastors and aren't young. It's been humbling to discover that it's been helpful for people from around the world. We don't claim to have "arrived" at anything we've discussed in the podcast, or now in this book. We still carry our insecurities, our weaknesses, and our sins. But with so many of you, we find that thinking through how gospel doctrine creates gospel culture cheers our hearts and provides fresh strength for our steps ahead. We're grateful to all of you who have reached out with feedback, encouragement, and questions.

We would like to express our gratitude to The Gospel Coalition, who first asked Ray to host a podcast for younger pastors. TGC has since produced and hosted *You're Not Crazy*, and they first gave us the idea of writing a book together based on those conversations. Two friends have been exceptional in their service to all of us: Andrew Laparra, who produces the podcast, and Jared Kennedy, who edited this book. Both have been cheerful, patient, and a joy to know. *They* have let their love for the Lord and his people be genuine! We thank Russell Moore for writing the foreword and Bishop Clark Lowenfield for writing the afterword. Both men are gospel stalwarts in this generation and dear friends to us. Finally, we thank our friends at Crossway for their outstanding partnership in getting this book now to you, our reader.

God be with you, friend.

General Index

trusting in emboldens us to fight
oppression, 12
truth of, xviii
ultimacy of, 11
welcome of in real time, 34–37
warning of concerning Scriptures
and eternal life, 78–79
Jobs, Steve, 101–2
justification, 2n2, 3, 4, 8–9, 10,
11–12, 14, 15, 19, 62, 126. *See
also* self-justification

King, Martin Luther, Jr., 102

leadership, 97–99
leadership
God's instructions for, 100–101
in Israel, 99–100
lessons for pastors concerning,
101–2
that takes, 99–100
three foundational truths of,
106–10
and what God forbids, 103–4
worldly models of, 101–3
leprosy, 35
Lincoln, Abraham, 101
Lloyd-Jones, Martyn, 6, 94–95
The Lord of the Rings (Tolkien), 49–50
love, 133–34
Lucas, Dick, 77
Luke, on growth of the church,
127–28
Luther, Martin, 2–3

Machen, J. Gresham, 11
Mandela, Nelson, 102
Mary, 87–89
mercy, 25–26
Miller, Donald, 43
Montgomery, B. L., 102

Moore, Russell, 71–73

New Testament, helpfulness to
church culture, 4

obedience, gospel vision as key to,
92–93

Palma Cathedral, 124
pastors
and attention to familial life of
church, 115–16
as CEO's, 102–3
ongoing growth of, 110–11
Paul, xvii, 6, 8, 12, 15, 24, 28, 42,
68, 82, 91
Paul
care of for people, 10–11
on care of widows, xvi
on Christ's second coming, 26
on dealing with the "weak in
faith," 105
on the definition of a church, 123
in Ephesus, 83–84
on false teachers, 15–17
on genuine love, 134
on God's ministry, 107
on hospitality, 38
on hypocrisy, 13–14
inadequacy of as public speaker,
80
on wisdom of God, 131
on welcoming others, 28–29
Peter, 12, 15
Peter
denial of Jesus by, 13
on hospitality, 37–38
hypocrisy of, 13–14
on the work and heart of an elder,
104–5
Pharisees, 7, 8, 79

Scripture Index

Also Available from the Gospel Coalition